Parent's Quick Start Guide to Dyscalculia

A Math Learning Disability

James W. Forgan and Noelle Balsamo

with Lisa A. Finnegan

Routledge
Taylor & Francis Group
NEW YORK AND LONDON

Designed cover image: Getty Images

First published 2026
by Routledge
605 Third Avenue, New York, NY 10158

and by Routledge
4 Park Square, Milton Park, Abingdon, Oxon, OX14 4RN

Routledge is an imprint of the Taylor & Francis Group, an informa business

© 2026 James W. Forgan and Noelle Balsamo

The right of James W. Forgan and Noelle Balsamo to be identified as authors of this work has been asserted in accordance with sections 77 and 78 of the Copyright, Designs and Patents Act 1988.

All rights reserved. No part of this book may be reprinted or reproduced or utilised in any form or by any electronic, mechanical, or other means, now known or hereafter invented, including photocopying and recording, or in any information storage or retrieval system, without permission in writing from the publishers.

Trademark notice: Product or corporate names may be trademarks or registered trademarks, and are used only for identification and explanation without intent to infringe.

ISBN: 9781032957456 (pbk)
ISBN: 9781003586326 (ebk)

DOI: 10.4324/9781003586326

Typeset in Palatino
by Apex CoVantage, LLC

Parent's Quick Start Guide to Dyscalculia

Written by experts who understand the science of dyscalculia as well as the pragmatic realities families face, *Parent's Quick Start Guide to Dyscalculia* provides parents and caregivers with the information they need and steps they can take to support and encourage their child.

This practical resource transforms complex terminology into accessible guidance. You'll find clear explanations that demystify dyscalculia, alongside expert insights on assessment procedures and what they reveal. Discover research-backed strategies to ease math anxiety, boost confidence, and make numbers less intimidating while learning to effectively advocate within school systems, develop tailored educational plans, and build productive partnerships with teachers and specialists.

From classroom accommodations to at-home learning techniques, this comprehensive guide equips you with everything needed to support your child's mathematical journey.

James W. Forgan is Associate Professor of Special Education at Florida Atlantic University where he prepares teachers to educate children with dyscalculia and related disabilities.

Noelle Balsamo is Adjunct Instructor at Florida Atlantic University and Independent Consultant supporting best practices in educating and parenting children with disabilities.

Dedication

James dedicates this book to Mr. Ramsey and Mr. Cooper who taught him a lot about numbers.

Noelle dedicates this book to her late father, her first helper in all things math.

Contents

About the Authors . . . . *viii*

Introduction. 1

1 Dyscalculia Explained. 3

2 Assessing for Dyscalculia. .17

3 Overcoming Math Anxiety and Increasing
  Self-Esteem 32

4 Math Teaching and Learning Strategies 42

5 Special Math Curriculum. .58

6 Strategies for Making Math Fun. 69

7 Math Accommodations 83

8 Math Technology. 100

9 Effective School Plans. 110

10 Collaborating With Professionals 126

About the Authors

Noelle Balsamo, Ed.D. is Adjunct Instructor at Florida Atlantic University and Independent Consultant, supporting best practices in educating and parenting children with disabilities. She is the co-author of *Parent's Quick Start Guide to Autism*, *Parent's Quick Start Guide to Dyslexia*, and *Parent's Quick Start Guide to Dysgraphia*.

James W. Forgan, Ph.D. is Associate Professor of Special Education at Florida Atlantic University, where he prepares teachers to educate children with dyscalculia and related disabilities. He is co-author of *The Impulsive, Disorganized Child: Solutions for Parenting Kids With Executive Functioning Difficulties*, *Stressed Out!: Solutions to Help Your Child Manage and Overcome Stress*, *Parent's Quick Start Guide to Autism*, *Parent's Quick Start Guide to Dyslexia*, and *Parent's Quick Start Guide to Dysgraphia*.

Lisa A. Finnegan, Ph.D. is currently Associate Professor in the Department of Special Education, supporting the preparation of both in-service and pre-service teachers to meet the needs of their students with exceptional needs and their families.

Introduction

"If you have $196 dollars and you spend $27, how much money remains?" If you are a math whiz you quickly knew the answer was $169, but perhaps you had to really think about it, write it, ask Alexa, or use a calculator before knowing the answer. The key here is you knew the basics of how to solve the problem. If you did not use technology, you could solve the math problem by hand.

Some children receive adequate math instruction but perform poorly in math due to a math learning disability called dyscalculia. These children might grasp simple math but struggle with multi-step math or math word problems. They learn multiplication facts only to forget them. As one child put it, "The numbers just fall out of my head."

There are many reasons why a child might have math difficulty. Consider the introductory math problem. What brain systems did you use to solve the problem? One cognitive system which is important for math is visualization. You might have visualized the numbers 196 and 27 in your mind as you visually regrouped and subtracted to solve the equation. Another important cognitive system is your working memory. You had to hold 196 and 27 in your working memory while you performed the math operation.

A third cognitive system important for math is attention. Regardless of using mental math or paper, you had to give great attention to detail as you solved the problem. If you made one careless error, it doomed your answer. Language is a fourth cognitive system involved in math. You had to use language to understand "how much money remains" requires subtraction. Math has other specialized vocabulary words such as sum, radius, integer, and hypotenuse. A fifth cognitive system needed for math is processing speed. Your child is often timed on math tests or expected to rapidly know their basic addition, subtraction, or multiplication facts. Slow processing speed limits your child's capacity for rapid math performance.

DOI: 10.4324/9781003586326-1

Thus, telling your child to "try harder" in math is not the solution when your child has dyscalculia. Psychoeducational or similar types of testing for your child can help identify which of your child's cognitive systems are working well and which ones might be causing a math learning disability and dyscalculia. There are specialized math programs and math learning strategies available to help children. In addition, your child might be eligible for classroom accommodations on a 504 Plan or specialized instruction and an Individual Education Program (IEP).

If teachers say, "Math might just not be your child's preferred subject" or "Your child just has to try harder," take that as a warning sign that more must be done to help understand your child's math challenges. Their words might be true, but remember you know your child best. Don't be afraid to ask for testing or seek out our own testing.

Time is a precious commodity, so if your child has dyscalculia, you want to maximize opportunities for improvement while minimizing barriers which hinder. We are pleased you found our book since that is our aim. This book provides you with quick, get-to-the-point evidence-based information to help your child. We guide you through the process of identifying dyscalculia, understanding treatments, obtaining accommodations, and supporting your child.

1

Dyscalculia Explained

Dyscalculia Explained

For many, a diagnosis of dyscalculia can be as difficult to comprehend as it is to pronounce (dis-kal-kool-ee-ah). Historically, dyscalculia has been overshadowed by more broadly recognized learning disabilities known to impact children's academic achievement in early stages of their schooling (e.g., dyslexia [reading disability], attention deficit hyperactivity disorder [ADHD]). So unsurprisingly, parents often report feeling completely "in the dark" when they first hear that their child's persistently poor math skills may be due to an underlying neurological condition known as *dyscalculia*, a Greek and Latin term that roughly, and somewhat misleadingly, translates to "badly calculating."

If you think this translation sounds overly simplistic for such a complex condition with an equally difficult-to-pronounce name, you are not alone! Parents commonly admit to feeling frustrated by the highly technical definitions and conflicting terminology they encounter when they first tentatively ask (or, worse, type!) the words "what is dyscalculia?" in an effort to better understand their child.

Steph, a mother of a newly diagnosed third grader, laments:

> I found a dozen blogs and online parent groups for children with dyslexia, but had to scroll through half the internet before I could find other parents like me who heard the word dyscalculia for the first time when I was told my daughter has it.

Others are only beginning to seek an explanation for their child's increasing distress with math and are not yet convinced that there is an underlying cause at all, let alone feel confident on what to call it! *Not everyone is "good at math,"* they think! "Isn't it just a lack of focus or motivation?" they ask. "I never liked math either," they say in their child's defense.

Jocelyn, a mother of a sixth grader shares:

> The closest explanation I could find for Jake's problems in my first internet searches was that he may be suffering with a form of *Number Dyslexia*, . . . so my first call was to a reading specialist, even though he has always been a pretty good reader. I didn't know dyscalculia was even something I should ask about!

Like Steph and Jocelyn, you may be finding it difficult to navigate through confusing information as you begin to explore this seemingly obscure diagnosis. However, rest assured you are in good company. Since Czechoslovakian psychologist Ladislav Kosc first introduced the term dyscalculia in 1974, much has been learned about the prevalence of school-aged children with dyscalculia, which is now estimated to be around 6 percent of the general population (Morsanyi et al., 2018). This estimation is similar to that of dyslexia and ADHD (Shalev et al., 2000), which may be surprising to some given that the latter are the more "talked about" disabilities in school-aged children.

You can also be assured that dyscalculia, and math learning disabilities in general, have received increased global attention and focused research since 2008 (Butterworth, 2018). As a result, you and your child will benefit from a number of helpful and up-to-date resources and supports that we will highlight for you in each chapter of this book. In this first chapter, we will help you make sense of the new language you will hear and steer you towards the facts you will need to know to best advocate for your child and away from the misconceptions you will want to avoid to protect your time and money.

The Language of Dyscalculia

Had the diagnostic community stuck with just the one term of dyscalculia, perhaps there would be less confusion amongst parents navigating this diagnosis for the first time. However, different diagnostic entities use different terminology (as well as different criteria) to determine if there is an underlying learning disability from which the concerning mathematical impairments manifest. This is discussed in more detail in Chapter 2. Here, we provide a brief explanation of the different terminology that you are likely to encounter in your discussions with various professionals across settings.

- **Mathematics Disorder:** A term used in the Diagnostic and Statistical Manual of Mental Disorders, fourth edition (DSM-IV)—a manual provided by the American Psychiatric Association (APA) in 1994 to inform diagnostic criteria for a number of neurodevelopmental disorders (inclusive but not limited to learning disabilities).
- **Specific Learning Disorder with Impairments in Mathematics:** This term replaced mathematics disorder in the most current Diagnostic and Statistical Manual of Mental Disorders, fifth edition (DSM-V) in 2013. Here, the disorder is defined as "difficulty learning academic skills related to math persisting for at a minimum 6 months despite adequate instruction targeting the area(s) of difficulty" (APA, 2013). This edition also specifies that the difficulties must present in the absence of other explanations (i.e., intellectual disabilities, visual or hearing impairments, mental disorders, neurological disorders, psycho-social difficulty, language differences).
- **Specific Learning Disability (SLD):** An educational term defined by the Individuals with Disabilities Education

Act [IDEA] of 2004 as "a disorder in one or more of the basic psychological processes that may manifest itself in the inability to listen, think, speak, read, write, spell, or to do mathematical calculations" (U.S Department of Education, 2004). SLD is one of the federally recognized categories of students eligible for special education services in the United States. This is discussed in greater detail in Chapter 9.

Do not let the many terms and acronyms distract you from what is most important! Like Brian Butterworth astutely states in his book *Dyscalculia: From Science to Education* (2019): "Dyscalculia is whatever your authorities and professionals think it is!" In other words, the goal is to identify the underlying cause of your child's challenges in order to access timely intervention that is individualized to meet their unique needs. So, for our purposes, we will use the term dyscalculia interchangeably throughout this book, as it is the simplest and most common way to refer to the challenges that have brought you to this resource (once one learns how to pronounce it!).

Dyscalculia and the Brain

It is important to understand that dyscalculia is more than just being "bad at math." Rather, it is a neurological condition characterized by persistent and pervasive weakness in number sense, memorization of basic math facts, and accurate and fluent calculation (APA, 2013). Or said another way, the core deficit of dyscalculia is the lack of an intuitive sense of numbers (Butterworth, 2018). Just as children with dyslexia (a reading disability) inherently lack the ability to identify and manipulate individual sounds within words (phonological awareness), the dyscalculic child struggles to identify and make sense of the relationship between numbers, each resulting in a lack of proficiency due to their respective core deficits.

As briefly mentioned in the introduction and discussed further in Chapter 2, there are a number of complex cognitive processes that contribute to overall proficiency in math and are impactful in the case of dyscalculia, including the following:

- Language (comprehension of written and spoken words)
- Visual Spatial (interpretation of spatial relationships)
- Visual Motor (coordination of visual information with motor actions)
- Working Memory (ability to hold, manipulate, and recall information)
- Executive Functioning (higher level cognitive skills that impact attention, processing speed, and organization)

Together, these processes serve as a kind of cognitive "tool kit" for higher-level mathematical thinking. As a result of these inherent neurological differences, you may observe some or all of the following common characteristics in your child with dyscalculia at different stages of their schooling:

Preschool
- Poor number identification skills
- Trouble learning to count
- Inability to recognize patterns
- Inability to associate a number to an object (one-to-one correspondence)

Elementary School
- Difficulty learning or recalling basic math facts
- Frequent calculation errors
- Inability to use mental math (e.g., relies on finger counting)
- Lack of recognition of mathematical symbols (e.g., +, −)
- Lack of recognition of mathematical terms (e.g., more, less, greater)
- Trouble with place value
- Trouble learning to tell time or understanding time as a measurement (e.g., We leave in 15 minutes.)

Secondary School
- Trouble remembering math concepts
- Difficulty with money
- Unable to read clocks
- Unable to read maps
- Trouble with math language and solving word problems
- Trouble keeping score
- Difficulty reading graphs and charts
- Difficulty estimating (time, distance, etc.)
- Inability to read maps
- General avoidance of math-related tasks

Keep in mind the dyscalculic brain is wired differently, not deficiently! Yes, a child with dyscalculia will acquire math-related skills differently and on a delayed timeline when compared to the general population of students. However, the science of dyscalculia is promising! Knowing the research that informs best practices in dyscalculia intervention will help you become an informed and lifelong advocate for your child.

What the Research Reports

In the scientific community, dyscalculia is classified as being either developmental (dyscalculia) or acquired (acalculia) based on the onset of occurrence. Developmental dyscalculia, as it is referred to in the scholarly literature, emerges in childhood and is understood to be congenital (existing at or before birth) (Butterworth, 2018). Based on this theoretical perspective, children with developmental dyscalculia are born with a biological propensity for the core numerical deficits that present later in life. It is theorized that developmental dyscalculia results from a combination of contributing factors (genetic predisposition, neurologic abnormalities, and environmental conditions) (Shalev & Gross-Tsur, 2001). On the other hand, acquired dyscalculia is attributed to an event that occurred later in life such as a traumatic brain injury or a cardiovascular event (e.g., stroke).

Although there is no consensus amongst researchers that developmental dyscalculia is definitively an inherited condition, a number of twin studies suggest inheritance is likely a contributing factor in some but not all cases. Further, pregnancy abnormalities such as preterm birth or disturbances to fetal development in-utero are correlated with higher rates of developmental dyscalculia in some studies, although this too is only a theoretical explanation at this stage of the science (Butterworth, 2018).

Causation research is helpful to discuss here only for the purpose of providing scientific evidence that developmental dyscalculia is indeed a neurobiological condition that necessitates focused intervention throughout the lifespan. It should also be emphasized here that, despite it being an inherent brain-based disorder, researchers repeatedly assert that developmental dyscalculia should not be characterized as a deficiency in intelligence. Nor should it be considered a fixed condition that is unresponsive to intervention. On the contrary, there is strong evidence supporting the benefits of early and focused intervention and numerous demonstrations of improved outcomes following diagnosis.

Several research groups have attempted to further classify dyscalculia into distinct subtypes to better characterize the differences observed between learners. However, there is little consensus in the professional literature about how to best characterize and describe subtypes of dyscalculia. This is explained, in part, by the limited range of skills assessed and the different diagnostic instruments used, as well as varying study design methods that lead to varying results across the collective studies (Kißler et al., 2021).

In 2021, Kißler and colleagues examined the body of research focused on subtype classification and proposed two potential subtypes based on level of severity: a slightly impaired subtype (subgroup 1) and a severely impaired subtype (subgroup 2). A notable distinction between these groups was the comorbidity of attention deficits, which were implicated as a significant contributing factor in the more profoundly impaired subtype. This finding has important implications, as it suggests a prioritized need to focus intervention for attention challenges in order to minimize the impact of dyscalculia across the lifespan.

Given the known core deficits in numeracy (ability to understand and use math in daily life) and number sense (an intuitive understanding of numbers), a high-quality intervention plan for dyscalculia should explicitly and systematically aim to build these capacities in a measurable and meaningful way. According to Butterworth (2018), it is imperative that instruction be

- based on the results of a careful diagnostic assessment of the learner's strengths and weaknesses;
- individualized to the learner's current level of understanding/performance;
- sequenced, teaching concrete information before progressing to abstract concepts or symbolic calculations;
- provide sufficient repetition to support retention of previously taught skills;
- supported by digital technologies that are adaptive and provide timely feedback; and
- an overall positive experience, especially in regards to arithmetic.

In a 2019 study published by Delgado and colleagues, the researchers identified a prioritized need to improve educational processes as a whole to better support dyscalculic learners. Specifically, they call for systemic adaptations to the learning environments that include differentiated assessment, segmented instruction based on cognitive pacing, and the use of innovative and didactic teaching materials that engage and motivate dyscalculic learners. They also call for a collaborative home and school approach where parents and specialists work together to improve individual student outcomes. See Chapter 4 for more information on teaching and learning strategies and Chapter 10 for more on effective collaboration.

It is important to note that it is common for both dyslexia and attention deficit hyperactivity disorder (ADHD) to co-occur with dyscalculia, due to the theoretical overlapping genetic risks (van Bergen, 2025). In a 2025 study, van Bergen and colleagues reported that children with ADHD were two times as likely to have dyscalculia, and children with dyslexia were three times as likely to have dyscalculia when compared to children without these respective conditions. Given the suggested correlation of co-occurring conditions, it is critical to have your child assessed in all impacted areas of learning and ensure that the plan for intervention reflects the identified strengths and weaknesses across academic domains when appropriate.

Quick Start Guide to Dyscalculia

Stick to the Facts. Although evolving, the science of dyscalculia is clear on the following:

- Dyscalculia *is* a biological condition of the brain
- Dyscalculia *is* a lifelong condition
- Dyscalculia *is* responsive to evidence-based targeted interventions
- Dyscalculia *is not* indicative of IQ or intelligence
- Dyscalculia *is not* merely a lack of focus, motivation, etc.
- Dyscalculia *is not* merely a lack of quality instruction
- Dyscalculia *is not* identical from person to person

The goal of this resource is to guide you towards the most up-to-date information and effective interventions for your child. Try to avoid pseudo-science, unsolicited marketed products, and unvetted online chat boards that may provide misleading information and distract you from putting your time and effort into what we know to be true and what works!

Know How Math Skills Add Up

Math itself is a complex construct even in the absence of neurological barriers with its own nuanced terminology. It would be helpful to know what is considered developmentally appropriate in math instruction and how it is sequentially taught in your child's school system. Knowing how math skills are conceptualized and categorized may help you better understand your child's unique strengths and challenges. Here we share a few concepts to make note of as you progress through your journey:

Pre-Number Skills. These are the basic skills children need to grasp in order to become proficient in more complex concepts as they progress through the math curriculum including the following:

- Number identification
- Shape identification
- Counting
- Sorting
- Matching
- Comparing

These skills are best supported through guided play activities. If you are a parent of a young child, you are likely already in possession of toys, books, and games that promote these skills. This is just a reminder to be mindful of opportunities to teach and reinforce these foundational skills, as they are as essential to school success as the ABCs.

Number Sense. In the simplest terms, number sense refers to one's ability to understand numbers and their relationships. A child that has strong number sense can think critically and intuitively about numbers, which sets the foundation for the development of arithmetic skills. Evidence of number sense includes the ability to do the following:

- Order numbers
- Differentiate quantities
- Understand what numbers represent
- Recognize relationships between numbers (e.g., greater than, less than)
- Comprehend the relative size of numbers (e.g., compare, estimate)

Practice counting, grouping, and regrouping objects with your child. Ask questions that help them to estimate, such as "how many Legos do you think are in this bin?" and compare quantities, "which pile do you think has more goldfish?" See the resource section of this chapter for more ideas on how you can help your child to see and talk about the relationship between numbers better.

Types of Math. The broad field of mathematics is divided into various branches with both discrete and overlapping skill sets. As you may recall, these are often divided into "subjects" and taught in a predetermined sequential order and most commonly include the following in most K–12 public school systems:

- Arithmetic (generally thought of the basic numerical operations of addition, subtraction, multiplication, and division, or the "manipulation" of numbers)
- Algebra (advanced arithmetic involving symbols [variables] to represent unknown numbers and solving for the unknown [equations])
- Geometry (concerns properties related to shapes and figures)
- Calculus (focuses on rate of change over time)
- Trigonometry (pertains to specific functions of angles)
- Statistics (deals with the collection and interpretation of data)

Make Math Matter

How often have you heard people say "when will I ever use this in real life?" or scroll across an internet meme joking that someone "survived another day without using algebra" or gloating that we are indeed "walking around with a calculator at all times in our pockets" despite pre-smart phone warnings that we could not rely on a machine to do math for us in "real life." Yes, math anxiety is real for many of us, and our past struggles can often lead to some amusing yet disparaging remarks on how important it even is to our daily life (see Chapter 3 for strategies to address math anxiety). However, as we emphasize throughout this book, mathematical competence is indeed essential to navigating modern life independently. In any given day we rely on numerical knowledge and computation skills to do the following:

- Pay bills
- Shop on a budget
- Follow recipes
- Manage time
- Navigate driving
- Play games and watch sports

As importantly, math skills are crucial to overall cognitive functioning (logical thinking, problem solving, pattern recognition, decision making, etc.) and is correlated with higher graduation rates, steady employment, and improved mental and physical health (Wilkey et al., 2020). So, it is important to model positive math attitudes and behaviors for your child. Chapter 6 will introduce you to a number of ways to make math fun and engage your child in positive experiences related to math. If a love of reading can be fostered through comforting home routines such as shared read-aloud activities and family trips to the library, then so can math!

Count on Others

Share this resource with friends and family who would benefit from having a deeper understanding of the challenges you and your child have been facing. Having a circle of support that acknowledges your child's learning disability and joins you in your efforts to advocate for the help they deserve will be a real asset along this journey.

Reach out to knowledgeable professionals who can determine your child's unique instructional needs and provide systematic evidenced-based interventions that target the core deficits that characterize dyscalculia. If you have not yet sought out a formal evaluation to confirm your suspicions that there is an underlying disability as the root of your child's math challenges, then we encourage you to do so after reading Chapter 2.

If your child has been found eligible for school-based services, we encourage you to embrace a team mindset that allows you to maintain a collaborative and solution-focused relationship with school staff. Chapter 10 will provide you with guidance on how to best collaborate with the professionals who can help you help your child.

Summary

Wherever you are on the diagnostic journey, it is important to have a foundational understanding of what dyscalculia is (a learning disability), as well as what it is not (something to be dismissed or grown out of), in order to become an informed advocate who can comfortably and confidently discuss your child's unique needs with the professionals who are poised and ready to help you both. As this is the ultimate goal of this guide, we begin in Chapter 1 by providing you with a brief explanation of how mathematical learning is generally conceptualized, as well as a broad description of how dyscalculia is commonly characterized and discussed across ages and settings. Keep reading to learn more about how you can work together with your child and qualified professionals to set them up for success now and in the future.

Resources

https://dictionary.cambridge.org/us/pronunciation/english/dyscalculia- Cambridge Dictionary

Learning Disabilities—Learning Disabilities Association of America- Dyscalculia and other Learning Disabilities

What is dyscalculia?—Understood.com

Building Students' Number Sense in Elementary Math | Edutopia—Edutopia

References

American Psychiatric Association. (2013). *Diagnostic and statistical manual of mental disorders: DSM-V* (Vol. 5). American Psychiatric Association.

Butterworth, B. (2018). *Dyscalculia: From science to education.* Routledge.

Delgado, M. A. C., Delgado, R. I. Z., Palma, R. P., & Moya, M. E. (2019). Dyscalculia and pedagogical intervention. *International Research Journal of Management, IT and Social Sciences*, *6*(5), 95–100.

Kißler, C., Schwenk, C., & Kuhn, J. T. (2021). Two dyscalculia subtypes with similar, low comorbidity profiles: A mixture model analysis. *Frontiers in Psychology*, *12*, 589506.

Morsanyi, K., van Bers, B. M., McCormack, T., & McGourty, J. (2018). The prevalence of specific learning disorder in mathematics and comorbidity with other developmental disorders in primary school-age children. *British Journal of Psychology*, *109*(4), 917–940.

Shalev, R. S., Auerbach, J., Manor, O., & Gross-Tsur, V. (2000). Developmental dyscalculia: Prevalence and prognosis. *European Child & Adolescent Psychiatry*, *9*(Suppl 2), S58–S64. https://doi.org/10.1007/s007870070011

Shalev, R. S., & Gross-Tsur, V. (2001). Developmental dyscalculia. *Pediatric Neurology*, *24*(5), 337–342.

U.S. Department of Education. (2004). Individuals with disabilities education act. *Public Law*, 108–446. https://www.congress.gov/bill/108th-congress/house-bill/1350/text

van Bergen, E., de Zeeuw, E. L., Hart, S. A., Boomsma, D. I., de Geus, E. J., & Kan, K. J. (2025). Co-Occurrence and causality among ADHD, dyslexia, and dyscalculia. *Psychological Science*, *36*(3), 204–217.

Wilkey, E. D., Pollack, C., & Price, G. R. (2020). Dyscalculia and typical math achievement are associated with individual differences in number-specific executive function. *Child Development*, *91*(2), 596–619.

2
Assessing for Dyscalculia

Assessing for Dyscalculia Explained

A concerned father once asked us, "What is the threshold for knowing if it's dyscalculia?" Currently there is no universal threshold for determining if low math performance is due to dyscalculia; however, as an informed parent you want to know more about your child's specific math struggle so you can begin corrective action. A thorough assessment for dyscalculia can confirm if your child has dyscalculia. So how do you locate a person to assess your child? Various professionals assess for dyscalculia, including clinical psychologists, school psychologists, and neuropsychologists. While many professionals can test your child, there is no stand-alone or sole definitive test or even a universal standard battery of tests used to diagnose dyscalculia. Thus, methods for assessing for dyscalculia vary. Some professionals might specifically assess for dyscalculia, whereas others assess your child for dyscalculia as one part of a larger evaluation process. Some professionals assess for dysgraphia, dyslexia, and dyscalculia learning disabilities at the same time.

Children use many cognitive systems during math, including

- critical thinking,
- self-talk,

TABLE 2.1 Professionals Evaluating for Dyscalculia

Professional	Type of Evaluation
School Psychologist, Clinical Psychologist, & Neuropsychologist	Depending on their experience and training: learning disabilities including dyscalculia, dyslexia, dyscalculia, ADHD, autism, and other related disabilities

- memory,
- attention,
- organization,
- sequencing,
- visual spatial thinking,
- fine motor coordination, and
- processing speed.

Since many cognitive areas are involved in math, the examiner should complete a broad assessment which encompasses most, if not all, of these areas. The examiner must rule out specific areas as the cause to identify the specific weaknesses. This helps guide treatment. Grace was a math tutor working with 10-year-old Miles. After a few months of minimal progress, Grace wondered if Miles had dyscalculia. He still transposed numbers, used his fingers to add and subtract, and he could not remember his multiplication tables. Miles seemed confused by math vocabulary and had difficulty applying logic to solve math problems. After a thorough evaluation, Miles' dyscalculia diagnosis was confirmed. Grace switched to the Math-U-See curriculum, and Miles started making slow progress. The evaluation unlocked understanding answers to help Grace best teach Miles.

The following are math and cognitive instruments from the broad areas involved during math which an examiner might use to assess for dyscalculia and math learning disabilities. Each area is followed by possible tests the examiner might use.

Math
- Woodcock Johnson Tests of Achievement subtests Calculation, Math Fluency, and Applied Math
- Wechsler Individual Achievement Tests subtests Numerical Operations, Math Problem Solving, and Math Fluency
- Kaufman Individual Achievement Tests subtests Math Concepts & Applications, Math Computation, and Math Fluency
- Test of Mathematical Abilities subtests Word Problems, Computation, Mathematical Symbols and Concepts, and Mathematics in Everyday Life
- Feifer Assessment of Mathematics ranges from nine to eighteen math subtests
- Test of Early Mathematics Ability contains formal and informal subtests

Visual Spatial Thinking
- Wechsler Intelligence Scale for Children subtests Visual Puzzles and Block Design
- NEPSY subtests Arrows, Geometric Puzzles, Block Construction
- Woodcock Johnson Tests of Cognitive Abilities Subtest Visualization and Picture Recognition
- Developmental Test of Visual Perception

Visual Motor Integration
- NEPSY II Design Copying
- Berry-Buktenica Developmental Test of Visual Motor Integration
- Bender Gestalt II

Intelligence
- Wechsler Intelligence Scale for Children
- Differential Ability Scales
- Reynolds Intellectual Assessment Scales

Working Memory
- Wide Range Assessment of Memory and Learning
- Wechsler Intelligence Scale for Children Working Memory Index
- Reynolds Intellectual Assessment Scales Working Memory Index

Executive Functioning: Attention, Processing Speed, Organization
- NEPSY Speeded Naming, Animal Sorting, Auditory Attention/Response Set, Inhibition subtests
- Delis-Kaplan Executive Functioning System Tower Test, Twenty Questions Test, Sorting Test
- Wechsler Intelligence Scale for Children Processing Speed subtests
- Woodcock Johnson Tests of Cognitive Abilities Processing Speed subtests
- RAN/RAS: Rapid Automatized Naming and Rapid Alternating Stimulus Tests
- Comprehensive Test of Phonological Processing Rapid Symbol Naming subtests
- Behavior Rating Inventory of Executive Function scale

If your child attends a public school, you may request for the school psychologist to test your child for dyscalculia. As discussed in Chapter 1, dyscalculia is also called a Learning Disorder in math or a Specific Learning Disability in math, depending on which diagnostic criteria are used. Thus, you can request an evaluation for any of these three areas: dyscalculia, Disorder of math, or a Specific Learning Disability in math. Provide a document describing the dyscalculia warning signs you observe as well as samples from any of the "do-it-yourself" informal screening assessments described in the Quick Start section on the following pages.

If your child attends a private school, you can bring your concerns to school staff to ask about any available evaluation resources. Many private schools have contracted psychologists that you can consult with about your concerns. If the school does not have any contractors, they might give you a list of reputable professionals who can provide a private dyscalculia evaluation.

How Classroom Teachers Assess for Math Difficulty

Your child's math teacher often uses an evaluation process called curriculum-based assessment (CBA). Curriculum-based assessment refers to models of assessment that emphasize a direct relationship to your child's curriculum. Teachers use CBAs in math to monitor and support students' progress, identify areas where they may need additional help, and make instructional decisions.

Your child's teacher might use repeated measures from the curriculum to evaluate the effectiveness of instruction and to adjust their instruction. This helps the teacher use more effective teaching methods and improve student achievement. A primary belief of CBA is that teachers should test what they teach.

When using a CBA, your child's teacher can monitor progress over time. For example, the teacher might give a weekly quiz or test covering fractions, to see if the students are mastering the material. These assessments give insight into which students are ready to move forward and which might need additional support or practice.

Some teachers use CBA to help differentiate instruction. CBAs help teachers differentiate math instruction based on individual student needs. Teachers may create various student groups based on the assessment results. For example, the teacher might design more challenging fractions work for students who excel and additional reteaching or practice for students who need more support.

Classroom-based assessment also helps your child's teacher identify your child's learning gaps. If your child struggles on a specific type of math problem, CBAs help the teacher pinpoint where the issue lies. For example, a student might understand basic addition of fractions but struggle with determining the least common denominator. By using CBAs, the teacher designs their instruction to address specific gaps in student understanding.

An example of a CBA is a weekly math quiz. If your child's teacher gives a short quiz every Friday covering the concepts taught during the week, that is a CBA. The teacher uses that information to know if your child is consistently struggling with a specific skill like adding fractions with different denominators. Based on that information, the teacher can provide additional practice before moving on to more complex topics like multiplying fractions.

Another CBA example is giving the students what teachers call an "exit ticket." At the end of a lesson the teacher asks students to complete an exit ticket with a math problem like: Solve: ¾ + ½=. The teacher quickly reviews the exit tickets to gauge if the students understand. If many students answer wrong, the teacher may decide to reteach the concept before moving on.

Technology can also be used as a CBM. Your child's teacher might use an interactive online tool like Kahoot or Quizizz, where students play a game that involves solving math problems. Your child's teacher receives immediate feedback about each child's correct and incorrect answers. If a certain type of question (like ordering fractions from smallest to largest) proves difficult for many students, the teacher can use the data to plan a review or reteaching. By incorporating CBAs into their teaching, math teachers can make decisions based on data rather than hunches to improve instruction and enhance student learning. In addition, CBA can provide data for your child's teacher to use to advocate for additional support for your child and other struggling students.

Response to Intervention or Multi-Tier System of Support
In addition to CBAs and testing by the school psychologist, many schools combine this information with a Response to Intervention or Multi-Tier System of Support process for evaluating for a math disability. One premise of this approach is to ensure your child's low math performance is not due to inadequate teaching. Some students might struggle in math because their teacher was ineffective, frequently absent, or did not use evidence-based math programs. Thus, the school-based team members will analyze available school-based data to show adequate evidence-based

instruction was provided to your child and your child did not make expected improvements.

The specifics for this vary by school, but there are some general principles for providing a multi-tier system of support. In the three-tiered triangle pictured in Figure 2.1, Tier 1 represents the general math curriculum that all students receive. Tier 2 has fewer students that receive additional math support in small groups. The top Tier 3 contains the fewest students that need the most intensive math support in small groups. Your child's math performance is frequently assessed throughout the process of providing increasing levels of support.

So, let's assume it's early November and your third-grade child is failing the general math curriculum assessments (Tier 1). The school-based team meets and decides your child needs additional math support in a small group (Tier 2). They also decide on one or more math goals for your child to work on. This might be, "Given a one-minute mixed addition and subtraction problem worksheet, the student will correctly answer 30 items on four out of five trials." The teacher then instructs and assesses your child for six to ten weeks. At that point, the team meets again to review data and progress. If your child does not improve, he is moved to Tier 3 which might include instruction in specialized

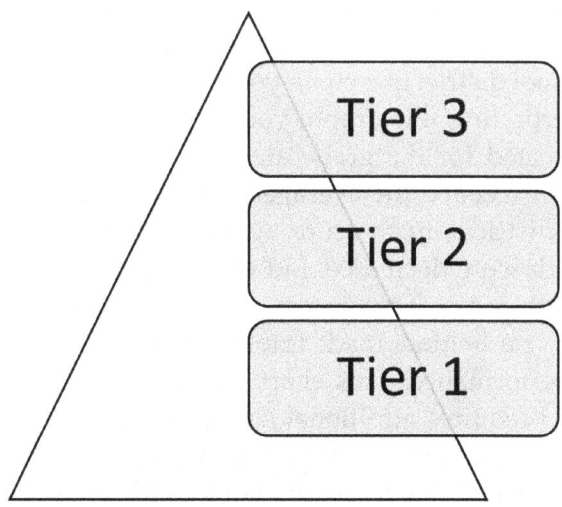

FIGURE 2.1 Three-Tier Triangle

math curriculum. Again, a goal will be established, the teacher will instruct, and data is collected. After another six to ten weeks, the team meets again.

If the assessments do not show adequate improvement (which is defined by the school-based team), the team will review any psychological testing, grades, and all available school-based data. Then your child might qualify for special education services and an IEP would be written. That is a lengthy process.

Interpreting Your Child's Math Results

It is fairly straightforward to understand your child's math performance when your child comes home with a letter grade on a math test. We've all attended enough school to know an A grade is the best and an F is the worst. However, it is often harder to decipher your child's math performance when you receive your child's progress monitoring math scores.

In Florida, the state where we reside, most schools use a progress monitoring approach for tracking students' performance. Students receive a computerized assessment in the fall, winter, and spring. This provides the teacher and you with three data points and insight regarding if your child is making "adequate progress." The school might send home a bar graph report such as seen later.

Your child's math growth is the bottom line, the growth of the average student in your child's grade is the middle line, and the overall school district growth in your child's grade is the top line. When interpreting this graph, your child's fall math score was below expected for the grade and district. Your child's winter math score exceeded the average grade score, but not the overall school district's math score. At the spring assessment, your child's math score decreased and was below both the grade and district math score. This summary implied your child started the school year behind, made improvement, and then decreased in math performance. This chart would support your child is behind and requires additional support. It's up to you and the teacher to determine which supports were provided between fall and winter testing that increased your child's math performance and could be reinstated.

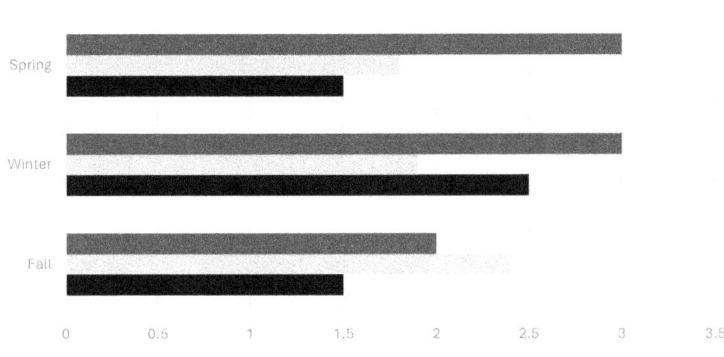

TABLE 2.1 Math Bar Graph Performance

Alternatively, you might receive a type of math report like the one later which contains numbers related to your child's math performance. Some of the scores appear easier to understand than others such as grade equivalent. Keep in mind that a grade equivalent score does not indicate mastery of curriculum. In the case later, it does not mean Charming's Math Applications ability is only at the first grade, fifth month skill level. A grade equivalent score indicates Charming answered the same number of items correct as a student in the first grade, fifth month. Let's assume this test had 40 items sequenced from easy to difficult. Both students answered 20 items correct and were given a 1.5 grade equivalent score. Keep in mind, Charming might have progressed in the test and answered number 40 correctly but missed many easier items due to careless errors. Thus, Charming clearly can complete higher math than the first grade, fifth month, but that is not reflected in the grade equivalent score. The takeaway point is that grade equivalent scores can be misleading.

Many teachers prefer reporting percentile scores as they are more stable scores and relatively straightforward to understand. A percentile score takes 100 students in your child's grade or of your child's age and ranks them. Picture a 100-step extension ladder extended into the sky. If your son's percentile score was 35, he would be on the 35th step, with 65 students scoring higher

TABLE 2.2 Math Scores Child's Name: Charming Student Child's Grade: 3

Math	Grade Equivalent	Age Equivalent	Percentile
Basic Math	2.8	8–3	37
Math Applications	1.5	7–0	21
Math Calculations	3.3	8–6	51

Note: Reach out right away to your child's school if they give you math performance data you don't understand.

than him. The average range for a percentile score is 25 to 75, with a score of 50 being the exact mean.

A visual analysis of the subsequent table shows Charming is lowest in Math Applications, so that would be the main area to provide supplemental math support.

What the Research Reports

Current research supports that if your child is struggling in math, it can be identified in early elementary school. While there are not as many math researchers as reading researchers, many have studied the early identification of math disabilities. Judge and Watson (2011) studied data from children kindergarten through fifth grade and reported, "We found a variation of students being diagnosed with LD at different grade levels even though they had lagged behind their peers since kindergarten" (p. 153). This supported findings from Mazzoco and Myers (2003), who reported persistent and poor math achievement was a primary characteristic of a math disability.

Mazzocco and Thompson (2005) studied whether cognitive data obtained during kindergarten could effectively predict which children will have a math learning disability in third grade. They also investigated if an abbreviated test battery could be as effective as a standard psychoeducational assessment at predicting a math learning disability. Their study reported an 80 percent success rate at predicting which children would have a math learning disability and that a screening was as successful as the standard full battery.

Fuchs et al. (2007) studied first- and second-grade students to predict a math disability. They used a multi-skill screener assessment including number identification/counting, fact retrieval, curriculum-based measurement computation, and curriculum-based measurement concepts/applications. While the screening approach was largely effective, it also missed some students who were later identified as having a math disability. Overall, they advocated that when trying to predict which students might have a math disability, a multi-skill screener was better to use than a single-skill screener.

There are various cognitive systems that contribute to a person's math ability that should be assessed. Mazzoco and Myers (2003) researched identifying math disabilities in elementary-age students. They used a combination of measures that assessed a child's IQ, math performance, visual spatial/perceptual performance, and reading-related skills. They advocated that evaluators should not simply use a single test to assess for math disabilities.

Kubas and colleagues (2014) researched using a cognitive strengths and weakness approach to identifying learning disabilities and to determine whether grouping children into specific MD subtypes using a processing strengths and weaknesses approach would help identify specific patterns of performance. Their research supported previous findings that weaker working memory, processing speed, and verbal comprehension contribute to poor math performance. Children with these weaknesses have slow automatic basic fact recall and rely on sequential processing rather than higher-level processing. This approach makes math very step by step with no overlap in mathematical operations. They also found students with math struggles rely upon associative learning, which means they learn by recognizing patterns, relationships, or properties that link various elements within mathematics.

According to dyscalculia researcher Brian Butterworth (2005), "There is an urgent societal need to help failing learners achieve a level of numeracy at which they can function adequately in the modern workplace" (p. 1053). Thus, using a comprehensive assessment approach to identifying dyscalculia and then supporting your child at an early age gives others understanding and a course for providing support.

Quick Start Guide to Assessing for Dyscalculia

Your intuition has told you it might be dyscalculia, and you read the dyscalculia warning signs in Chapter 1. Now you can try some informal and at-home, "do-it-yourself" types of screening assessments to further your insight that your child's struggle could be dyscalculia. Record your concerns on Table 2.3.

Review your responses from Table 2.3. If you checked off three or more, consider obtaining a formal dyscalculia assessment. Bring this book to your appointment or take a picture of the table to use to share your specific concerns. Use this specific information to start the assessment process. Help awaits.

TABLE 2.3 Dyscalculia Concerns Checklist

Informal Dyscalculia Assessment	No Concern	Yes Concern
1. Does your child despise math?		
2. Does your child have difficulty remembering basic math facts?		
3. Does your child still use fingers to compute math problems?		
4. Does your child have difficulty remembering coin values and understanding money?		
5. Is your child confused with differences in similar math vocabulary such as add, sum, compute?		
6. Does your child have difficulty solving math word problems even if the problem is read to them?		
7. Does your child have difficulty remembering math sequences such as steps in long division?		

Note: Does your child individually count a set of items instead of being able to count them by sight even if there are only five items?

Here are additional points and activities to consider to informally assess your child for dyscalculia. Of course, consider your child's age as the difficulty degree of these activities vary.

- Does your child struggle to understand basic number concepts such as understanding the value of numbers (e.g., not understanding that 25 is greater than 15).
- Ask your child to count in order, and observe if they mix up the order of numbers.
- Does your child struggle to memorize basic math facts or take a long time to recall simple math facts, even after repeated practice? Give your child a pop quiz on some basic math facts.
- Present different vocabulary such as "What is 3 + 4?" vs. "How many is 3 + 4?" Does your child have difficulty understanding?
- Provide a piece of notebook paper and ask your child to set up a math problem such as 240 + 137.
- Observe any struggles to align numbers with the proper place value when writing them.
- Ask your child to read a clock, especially an analog clock, and say the time. Ask your child to state the time at "quarter past" or "half past" on the clock.
- Generate a math word problem such as, "Samantha has 12 apples. She gives 4 apples to her friend, Emma. Then, she buys 6 more apples from the store. How many apples does Samantha have now?" Present this to your child and observe if they have difficulty understanding the question or how to extract math information from the text. Did your child struggle to organize information or figure out the steps needed to solve the problem?
- Try some mental math with your child and observe if they have difficulty holding the numbers in memory.
- Does your child often blame their poor math performance on "just being bad in math?"

If you see signs of dyscalculia, discuss these concerns with a professional or your child's teacher. Present your list of observations. An evaluation is needed if your concerns combine with your child's failing math grades.

Summary

Dyscalculia can be assessed in children as young as at least halfway through kindergarten, but it often takes an astute parent to bring specific concerns to the school's attention. It's also helpful for you to quantify your concerns by completing informal activities with your child. This provides data to help validate your intuitive concerns. There are psychologists, educators, and specialists waiting to help your child.

Resources

www.Amazon.com: Math practice workbooks for kids
www.MathFactsPro.com: Subscription based website for teachers and schools
www.math-drills.com: Free printable math fact sheets

References

Butterworth, B. (2005). Developmental dyscalculia. In *The handbook of mathematical cognition* (pp. 455–467). Psychology Press.

Fuchs, L. S., Fuchs, D., Compton, D. L., Bryant, J. D., Hamlett, C. L., & Seethaler, P. M. (2007). Mathematics screening and progress monitoring at first grade: Implications for responsiveness to intervention. *Exceptional Children, 73*(3), 311–330.

Judge, S., & Watson, S. M. (2011). Longitudinal outcomes for mathematics achievement for students with learning disabilities. *The Journal of Educational Research, 104*(3), 147–157.

Kubas, H. A., Schmid, A. D., Drefs, M. A., Poole, J. M., Holland, S., & Fiorello, C. A. (2014). Cognitive and academic profiles associated with math disability subtypes. *Learning Disabilities: A Multidisciplinary Journal*, *20*(1).

Mazzocco, M. M., & Myers, G. F. (2003). Complexities in identifying and defining mathematics learning disability in the primary school-age years. *Annals of Dyslexia*, *53*, 218–253.

Mazzocco, M. M., & Thompson, R. E. (2005). Kindergarten predictors of math learning disability. *Learning Disabilities Research & Practice*, *20*(3), 142–155.

3

Overcoming Math Anxiety and Increasing Self-Esteem

Math Anxiety Explained

Math is a stressor for many people. If you don't consider yourself a math person, then as an adult, you might leave budgeting to your spouse. Sure, you understand money concepts, but why keep track of every penny? Budgeting might stress you out. How about making change on the spot? Many adults simply use a debit card so they do not have to deal with the pressure of calculating if they give or receive the correct change when paying with cash. Likewise, you know income taxes are due every year, but doing them yourself is a nightmare, so you hire a professional. As adults we develop ways to work around our math weaknesses. Without a formal dyscalculia diagnosis needed to receive accommodations, our children must face math head on. This creates stress.

What Is Stress?

Stress is usually caused by something happening outside of you. Stress is your body's response to the demands and pressures that are experienced each day that can upset our normal balance. Our body functions best when it's at homeostasis: balanced and feeling good. When your child feels stress his body starts the "fight or flight" response, which is part of the sympathetic nervous system. Imagine your child is in math class and the teacher announces, "We are having a pop quiz today. You'll have ten minutes to complete the quiz and then I'll teach a new math unit." Your child's body releases the stress hormones of adrenaline and cortisol. His breathing speeds up, heart beats faster, and his muscles tense. He thinks, *I only have ten minutes. I can't do that, it's impossible!* When this occurs, your child cannot perform to his potential. His body is in an alert, reactive mode rather than a relaxed cognitive mode that allows higher-level thinking.

Your child must wait until his parasympathetic nervous system helps calm his body level down. His breathing, heart rate, and energy use all return to normal. His hormone levels drop. His mind relaxes. His body's "storm" is over and the sunshine returns. Unfortunately, this process took ten minutes. The result? He fails the test even though he might have known the material.

What Is Anxiety?

Anxiety comes from inside you. It is an unpleasant feeling from your thoughts and fears regarding apprehension that alerts you to a potential threat that is real or anticipated. Anxiety can happen without a clear cause. Individuals with high anxiety show activation in the amygdala area of their brain which is an area associated with processing negative emotions. This activation occurs with reduced activity in the intraparietal sulcus which is the brain structure critical to numerical processing.

Once activated, anxiety can even linger even after the stressor (e.g., math test) is finished. Your child keeps thinking and worrying about failing in math even when there is no math test. It's a feeling of nervousness that does not easily go away.

There is general anxiety as well as specific types of anxiety such as test anxiety, social anxiety, separation anxiety, and others. Your child might experience more than one type of anxiety. She might experience math anxiety as well as general anxiety about her school performance by comparing herself to her peers. You might have heard your child express that they are not smart enough or sometimes feel dumb.

As a parent, you can help your child by

- using care to not project any of your math anxiety onto your child,
- perceiving math challenges accurately,
- developing effective solutions to math struggles, and
- maintaining a global perspective.

Help your child understand math anxiety can be temporary. Discuss that different teachers teach math in various ways and perhaps the method your current child's math teacher is using is not the right fit. Next year's teacher or even the "right" math tutor can help reduce math anxiety and increase skill. Reassure your child that they are not destined to be bad at math.

Explain to your child the math anxiety they feel is nervousness, fear, or worry that makes them feel stressed, confused, or even scared when solving math problems or even thinking about math. Assure your child they are not alone. In fact, many people relate to math anxiety, even the late musician Jimmy Buffett in his song *Math Suks*. When it comes to math, his lyrics capture the sentiment of many adults and children alike.

What the Research Reports

For decades researchers have studied math anxiety as it is a multifaceted phenomenon.

In 1957, Dreger and Aiken studied college individuals and found number anxiety, noting that this was the students' emotional reaction to math. Researchers such as Ashcraft (2019), Hembree (1990) have summarized models for test anxiety, including the inference model and the deficit model. In the inference model, test anxiety disrupts recall of prior knowledge which results in lower test scores. In the deficit model, lower test scores are presumed due to poor study habits and deficient test taking skills.

Ramirez et al. (2018) proposed the disruption account theory in which math anxiety disrupts math performance by decreasing a person's working memory capacity which is needed for effective math performance. Additional math anxiety theories are the reduced competency theory, which suggests initial low math performance leads to math anxiety, and the processing efficiency theory, in which math anxiety impairs math performance by diverting one's cognitive resources (Ahmed et al., 2012).

Cipora et al. (2022) distinctly outline what we know about math anxiety, and their first point was, "Math anxiety exists—it cannot be reduced to other constructs" (p. 11). In other words, generalized anxiety, test anxiety, social anxiety, etc. are different from math anxiety. They also indicated math anxiety is distinct from students who simply have low math performance. Furthermore, students with and without dyscalculia experience math anxiety.

Overall, there are no meaningful gender differences in math performance, and males and females have equal aptitude for mathematics (Spelke, 2005). Yet, females consistently show higher levels of math anxiety (Cipora et al., 2022; Devine et al., 2012; Hembree, 1990; Hill et al., 2016). Two possible explanations are that females experience higher anxiety in general and that females more accurately self-report math anxiety as compared to males; however, the exact reasons are unclear.

Treatments for math anxiety vary. Hembree (1990) studied classroom interventions including curricular changes such as special classwork, computers, calculators, tutorials, small group, and self-paced instruction. He reported these, along with whole class psychological treatments, were not effective. What were effective treatments in reducing math anxiety were out-of-class psychological treatment. Systematic desensitization (exposing a person little by little to that which they are afraid of) with anger management and inhibition training was effective, as was cognitive restructuring combined with relaxation training.

Asanjarani and Zarebahramabadi (2021) studied 8- to 12-year-old male students with high mathematics anxiety and low mathematics self-concepts to determine if cognitive behavioral therapy (CBT) was an effective treatment. Students in the treatment group received once-a-week 90-minute group sessions for 12 weeks. The results showed participants in the treatment group reported lower math anxiety levels and a higher level of mathematics self-concept after the experiment. Thus, the cognitive restructuring challenged the child's irrational thinking and replaced them with more rational thinking.

Preventing math anxiety is equally important to treating math anxiety. Furner and Duffy (2022) write, "Some educators believe that teachers and parents who are afraid of math can pass on math anxiety to the next generation, not genetically, but by modeling behaviors of their own discomfort with the subject" (p. 3). Parents can monitor their own math attitudes and how they might verbally spread them to their child. Additional prevention strategies include providing young students with high levels of math success, learning how to apply different math strategies before the math activity, and regularly discussing students' math feelings and attitudes.

Quick Start Guide to Alleviating Math Anxiety

A first step to helping your child is understanding their disposition and feeling about math. Consider having your child or student complete the math survey provided here.

Directions:
Please answer the following questions honestly. There are no right or wrong answers. This is to help us understand how you feel about math.

Ask your child or student to respond to these open-ended questions.

1. What is your favorite part of doing math?
2. What makes you feel worried or nervous about math?
3. What would help you feel better about doing math?

After reviewing the responses, consider teaching your child how to recognize and understand what their body is telling them. Discuss the signs your child might experience, including

- heart beating fast,
- hands sweating,

TABLE 3.1 The Way I Feel About Math

Item			
The way I feel about math is:	Good	Bad	Neutral
How well can you memorize math facts?	Good	Bad	Neutral
How do you feel when you have to do math problems in class?	Good	Bad	Neutral
How do you feel when you get a math test or quiz?	Good	Bad	Neutral
How do you feel when the teacher asks you to answer a math question in front of the class?	Good	Bad	Neutral
The way I feel about doing math homework is:	Good	Bad	Neutral
When I prepare for a math test I feel:	Good	Bad	Neutral
I believe I can improve my math skills.	Yes	No	Unsure
Working with a math tutor/teacher helps me.	Yes	No	Unsure
Using a calculator helps me feel better about solving math problems.	Yes	No	Unsure

- faster breathing, and
- head pressure.

Next, teach tools to help cope with these feelings. Implement strategies to reduce math anxiety, such as reading books, offering more reassurance, using games to make math fun, or providing more individual support.

The following children's literature books are available on Amazon. Reading a book with your child helps give your child the understanding they are not alone in their math struggle. Children usually relate well to a book's central character. We recommend following a structure such as the following:

- Seat your child next to you and read the book to your child. You want your child to listen to the content and examine the pictures rather than reading.
- Periodically pause to discuss the character's concerns.
- Ask your child if they have ever felt that way.
- Discuss how the character solved their problem.
- Ask your child if they could use the same strategy.
- Discuss and practice when and how they would apply the strategy.

- Periodically reread the book to keep the strategy fresh in your child's mind.

No Math Today by Tiffany Michelle—This book follows Savannah's journey through the world of fractions, highlighting resilience, confidence, and relatable examples for kids on how to use math in day-to-day life.

I'm Trying to Love Math by Bethany Barton—This is a funny book that teaches kids to think differently about math and introduces examples of how people use math in really cool ways to help them realize math is about everyday life.

The Math Allergy by Melisa Lazarus—A great book to help kids realize they are not alone in their fears and anxiety about math and valuable ways to shift their mindset regarding math.

Fractions in Disguise by Edward Einhorn—A fun, engaging approach to fractions with a great storyline and illustrations.

I Can Be A Math Magician by Anna Claybourne—A colorful activity book that is great for students grade 8–12 and great for STEM and STEAM education/activities whether in the classroom or homeschooling setting.

A Place for Zero by Angeline Sparagna LoPresti—A playful story that helps introduce multiplication and number placement to kids in a fun way.

The Greedy Triangle by Marilyn Burns—A picture book that will introduce kids to basic math concepts and shapes.

Math Curse by Scieszka and Smith—A story of helping children overcome math anxiety.

A Gebra Named Al by Isdell—This book is about a middle school girl named Julie in the Land of Mathematics and her struggle with mathematics.

Change Your Child's Mindset

When your child has dyscalculia, it is understandable she does not enjoy math, but she can develop the mindset that she can still "do" math. Your child's math mindset is the way they think about their ability to solve math problems. A positive math mindset

TABLE 3.2 Types of Mindsets 1

Fixed Mindset	Growth Mindset
"I'm not good at running."	"I'm getting better each time I run."
"I'll never be a fast runner."	"I can work to become faster."
"Running is just not my thing."	"I have what it takes to be a runner."

TABLE 3.3 Types of Mindsets 2

Fixed Mindset	Growth Mindset
"I'm bad at math"	"I'm still learning math."
"This math makes no sense."	"I don't understand yet but I'll keep trying."
"I make too many mistakes."	"I can learn from my mistakes."

influences your child's math attitude, confidence at solving math problems, and even their willingness to attempt math.

There are two types of mindsets: a fixed mindset and a growth mindset. As you reflect on your child's responses to the math attitude survey, consider if they point to a fixed or growth math mindset. Discuss these with your child and provide examples from your own life. For example, you might discuss how you do not enjoy running for exercise. Explain that if you had a fixed mindset you might tell yourself the fixed mindset statements in Table 3.1. Then contrast this with growth mindset statements you could tell yourself.

Discuss the subsequent fixed and growth math mindset examples with your child. Ask your child which mindset they mostly maintain. Explain the growth mindset includes positive self-talk which helps us believe we can improve and learn and to try and maintain this mindset during math work.

Additional activities that can help reduce math anxiety include the following:

- Asking your child to say or write positive affirmations:
  - "I can do math."
  - "Math and I are becoming better friends."

- "Solving math correctly is more important than doing it quickly."
- Apply relaxation training by learning to breathe deeply before math tasks. Teach your child the 4–5–6 approach to breathe in deeply while counting to four, hold the breath while silently counting from one to five, and slowly breathe out as they count from one to six.
- Use relaxation techniques like visualizing success or listening to soft, calming music.
- Draw a "math monster" to show what math anxiety feels like, then imagine defeating it or scribbling it out using dark ink.

Summary

Math anxiety is real, a separate type of anxiety, and has been studied for decades. Boys and girls experience math anxiety, with more girls self-reporting math anxiety, which leads to the perception that more girls experience math anxiety. There are prevention and treatment approaches for math anxiety, including using cognitive behavior therapy, exposure therapy, skill training, and mindset training. To overcome math anxiety a combination of approaches works best along with experiencing high levels of math success.

Resources

AAAmath.com—Interactive math lessons for students in kindergarten through eighth grade.

Coolmath4kids.com—Math games for students in kindergarten through sixth grade.

Girlsrockmath.org—STEM camps for elementary to middle school girls.

Learning to Love Math: Teaching Strategies That Change Student Attitudes and Get Results by Judy Willis.

Math Anxiety Rating Scale (MARS) by Suinn & Winston.

References

Ahmed, W., Minnaert, A., Kuyper, H., & Van der Werf, G. (2012). Reciprocal relationships between math self-concept and math anxiety. *Learning and Individual Differences*, *22*(3), 385–389.

Asanjarani, F., & Zarebahramabadi, M. (2021). Evaluating the effectiveness of cognitive-behavioral therapy on math self-concept and math anxiety of elementary school students. *Preventing School Failure: Alternative Education for Children and Youth*, *65*(3), 223–229.

Ashcraft, M. H. (2019). Models of math anxiety. In *Mathematics anxiety* (pp. 1–19). Routledge.

Cipora, K., Santos, F. H., Kucian, K., & Dowker, A. (2022). Mathematics anxiety—where are we and where shall we go? *Annals of the New York Academy of Sciences*, *1513*(1), 10–20.

Devine, A., Fawcett, K., Szűcs, D., & Dowker, A. (2012). Gender differences in mathematics anxiety and the relation to mathematics performance while controlling for test anxiety. *Behavioral and Brain Functions*, *8*, 1–9.

Dreger, R. M., & Aiken, L. R., Jr (1957). The identification of number anxiety in a college population. *Journal of Educational Psychology*, *48*(6), 344.

Furner, J. M., & Duffy, M. L. (2022). Addressing math anxiety in a STEM world: Preventative, supportive, and corrective strategies for the inclusive classroom. *European Journal of STEM Education*, *7*(1), Article 11. https://doi.org/10.20897/ejsteme/11892

Hembree, R. (1990). The nature, effects, and relief of mathematics anxiety. *Journal for Research in Mathematics Education*, *21*(1), 33–46.

Hill, F., Mammarella, I. C., Devine, A., Caviola, S., Passolunghi, M. C., & Szűcs, D. (2016). Maths anxiety in primary and secondary school students: Gender differences, developmental changes and anxiety specificity. *Learning and Individual Differences*, *48*, 45–53.

Ramirez, G., Shaw, S. T., & Maloney, E. A. (2018). Math anxiety: Past research, promising interventions, and a new interpretation framework. *Educational Psychologist*, *53*(3), 145–164.

Spelke, E. S. (2005). Sex differences in intrinsic aptitude for mathematics and science?: A critical review. *American Psychologist*, *60*(9), 950.

4

Math Teaching and Learning Strategies

Math Teaching and Learning Strategies Explained

Amelia is a second grade student who struggles with math. She has just finished her breakfast, and her dad asks her to help him pack her lunch and snacks for the day. Amelia's dad hands her a container and tells her to count ten grapes. As she takes each grade he counts with her up to 10. Next he gives her a box of ABC crackers and a half cup measuring cup and tells her to scoop out two half cups for her morning and afternoon snack. He fills up her water bottle, and as Amelia places her snacks in her lunchbox her dad tells her to pick out one milk or juice carton. When her dad reaches for the bread to make her sandwich he notices there is only one slice, so he tells Amelia they must leave 20 minutes earlier than their regular time of 8:10 to run into the grocery store to pick up a small sub sandwich for her. Once Amelia and her dad are at the grocery store checkout line, he hands Amelia a $20 bill to pay for the sandwich and tells her this is $20. Then he tells Amelia the sandwich is $4.59. Amelia's dad says, "The sandwich is almost $5 and you have $20. Do you have enough?" Amelia responds yes. Then he asks if she will get change back from the cashier. Amelia hesitates, so her dad says, "If the sandwich is almost $5 let's count by fives to 20." They count together, and Amelia tells her dad yes, that she will get some money back. As they arrive at school her dad pulls up to the car line at 8:30 and tells Amelia, "Perfect timing. Leaving the house 20 minutes early allowed us to get the rest of your lunch and arrive at school on time."

Math is everywhere around you! It is in every part of your home, at the grocery store, restaurants, local parks, and even on your commute taking your child to school or anywhere in your community and beyond. Number sense and operations, fractions, algebraic reasoning, measurement, geometric reasoning, and data analysis and probability are all mathematical concepts that can be infused throughout the day-to-day activities that occur in our homes and community. Along with the daily learning of mathematical concepts in and around the home and extended community, parents can support their children's mathematical concept learning using effective strategies or techniques.

Strategies in teaching are the techniques and methods teachers use to deliver the content to their students. In most elementary and secondary classrooms, math and science content areas are often taught using what is known as implicit instruction or inquiry-based instruction. Implicit instruction is an approach to learning where students are exposed to a concept through discovery or exploration with the expectation that they will understand the concept through the materials they used. If you have heard of the recent discussions on the "science of reading," then you will understand that this idea of being exposed to words does not make a student a reader. Inquiry-based instruction is a similar approach to learning where teachers provide "big ideas" or key questions to students that they explore, make hypotheses, and attempt to discover a way to test their hypothesis and develop an understanding of the question concepts to come up with an answer. While this instructional approach may work for many typically developing students, it is not an effective approach for students who may have difficulty understanding those key overarching questions or how to develop and test a hypothesis. Students who struggle to learn through implicit instruction or inquiry-based instruction need instruction that is well-designed.

Explicit instruction is a well-researched effective instructional strategy used in special education and for students who struggle or are at risk of failing. Just as it sounds, explicit instruction is clear, focused, and direct. Explicit instruction focuses on the critical content to be learned which is broken down into smaller instructional chunks, sequenced, and connected to the pre-skills the student knows or needs to know to understand the content to be taught, follows a step-by-step modeling of the skill, and engages the student in the process of learning through active engagement during guided practice. Explicit instruction is structured and systematic. It is used to teach the what of the curriculum—what the teacher wants your child to know.

How your child learns the content and applies what they learn is done through learning strategies. These strategies are implemented to help students develop their thinking (cognitive) and analyze their thinking (metacognitive). This can be done through instructional enhancements and frameworks such as

- differentiated instruction—teachers tailor the lesson to meet learners various levels of needs;
- universal design for learning—teachers proactively adjust lessons to ensure learners have access to content, are motivated, challenged, and engaged (think of ramps for buildings [universal design] but for learning, a.k.a. curriculum);
- cooperative learning—structured group learning;
- peer-assisted learning—structured partnered learning; and
- strategy instruction.

Strategies in learning are the techniques or methods teachers use to help students to learn the content or a skill they need in the way they need to. Think of a strategy you might use to remember the list of grocery items that you left sitting on the counter. Do you try to visualize the written list to see if you can recall the items down the list, or think about what you're going to make for dinners during the week and what ingredients are needed or go aisle by aisle for hopeful recognition of the items on the list when you see them on the shelves? Your grocery list was your first strategy similar to taking notes or completing a graphic organizer in class, while your backup strategy might be visualization.

Strategies are tools we can use well beyond the classroom. You most likely still employ several strategies you learned in your own K12 education today. Think of the phrase "measure twice, cut once," or creating a task analysis for a home project or work assignment or even the strategy you learned to remember the names of the planets or the continents for Trivia Game night.

What the Research Reports

Early childhood centers spend the majority of the academic day focused on early literacy skills, leaving a reduced amount of structured academic learning time focused on early numeracy or potentially early numeracy learning occurring through non-structured instruction. Likewise, in our homes we spend time on early literacy skills through reading stories, singing the alphabet song, talking to our children about the letters in their name, and the letters in their environment (M for McDonald's and P for Publix). We may remember to count with our child as they blow bubbles or we hand them crackers, but more often than not the focus of the world around us is teaching our children to read. Extending and enhancing school-aged children's experiences with math outside formal school settings is believed to have the potential to improve math achievement (Nelson et al., 2024). A study examining home literacy and numeracy experiences on reading and math outcomes for children in kindergarten and first grade found that parent literacy teaching (e.g., letter names) predicted early math achievement as strongly as parent numeracy teaching (Manolitsis et al., 2013). In another study, Sheldon and Epstein (2005) found that home learning activities consistently and significantly related to children's higher math achievement after examining several family and community involvement activities across elementary and high school (Nelson et al., 2024). For students with dyscalculia or other disabilities, providing additional math practice at home is paramount to a child's success (Fong et al., 2024).

Your own experience with learning mathematics can play a role in supporting the learning of mathematics for your child. While it is not expected that you teach your child a brand new concept in mathematics it is important to keep in mind that children with dyscalculia may not have fully understood and retained all aspects of a newly learned mathematical concept. Similar to examining math anxiety comes the need to understand one's growth mindset, or lack of, regarding learning mathematics as that may transfer similarly to a child. When children believe they have the ability to learn difficult mathematical concepts even when they have made errors, they are likely to continue to persist in understanding and skill development (Dweck, 2019). Fong et al. (2024) recommend caregivers have a positive math experience with their child. This can be done by sharing with your child that math is everywhere, concepts build upon one another, mistakes are for learning, and some skills take more practice than others, just like when they learned to ride a bicycle.

The Benefits of a Growth Mindset

Where does the growth mindset fit into math teaching in the home? To begin, parents' modeling a growth mindset to their children through trial and error of approaches and strategies, persisting in understanding and explaining a concept, or providing scaffolded support with homework or incomplete daily class assignments reinforce the need for persistence and a belief that in the end understanding of what was previously learned in the classroom will occur. Since math is everywhere around you, mathematical discourse can be weaved throughout daily conversations in the home from early childhood through adulthood. Secondly, since mathematics concepts build upon one another (Bryant, 2021), for example, children must understand numbers and their values before they can understand greater or less than and children with dyscalculia are observed to math difficulties as early as preschool (Codding et al., 2016), introducing, discussing, and "playing" with math concepts in the home early in a child's life can build the background knowledge needed to support classroom math learning in the school years.

Benefits of Strategy Instruction

As children gain skills, teachers model and provide instruction on how to use specific learning strategies that support the acquisition of a new concept and build toward becoming more fluent in their responses to solving computation or word problems. Learning strategies have been used for decades to support students in mathematics. An example of this was a strategy I learned to spell the word "arithmetic" when I was in kindergarten from my best friend who had an older sibling and taught me the strategy of the first letter for each word of the sentence, "A rat in the house might eat the ice cream." This sentence strategy has helped me to write the word arithmetic since kindergarten, even as a struggling reader in K-2 grade. When students understand and use strategies, they have been taught in the classroom they make connections to their thinking about a concept. Strategies must first connect to the mathematical concept being learned but then must also be taught, modeled, practiced, and reviewed to be the most effective (Patti et al., 2021). To determine if your child would benefit in using a learning strategy, observe the way they solve mathematics computation and word problems.

According to the research, learning strategies must be automatic to be useful tools for students (Deshler et al., 1981; Deshler & Schumaker, 1986), particularly when students find a content challenging. Just as your child would need to know their math facts, they must also know the learning strategy like the back of their hand to be able to use the learning strategy to help them to address various mathematics computations and problems. The strategy must be explicitly taught step by step. It should be modeled by you to show them how it works and then the student should practice the strategy with guidance until memorized. Additionally, you will want to check on your child to verify that they are using the learning strategy correctly and that it is a helpful tool for them. Mnemonic strategies are one type of learning strategy.

Quick Start Guide to Using Math Learning and Learning Strategies

Be Observant Together

Observe your child as they work on math computation or math word problems. Do you see them strategically working through the problem? Ask them questions, such as, "How did you arrive at that answer?" "What did you do to solve that problem?" "Tell me how you got that answer?" These questions will help you gain insight into whether or not your child uses any strategies currently and how well they use a strategy. This math talk is an opportunity to learn what and how they are thinking as they try to solve computation or word problems.

After observing your child for the strategies they use, review the strategies later to identify other strategies that may assist them in math computation and problem solving. Remember these strategies should be explained, modeled, practiced, and monitored to ensure that your child is implementing them correctly and that they are truly helpful for them.

Test Strategies Out Together

CRA/CSA Strategy

This multisensory strategy involves initially using concrete objects to show the number, value, or a concept in math in a physical form. Concrete (C) representation of a concept should always be done when learning a new concept or to verify students' understanding of a new concept taught during the day if helping with homework. After children gain understanding with physical concrete objects they are typically ready to move on to visual representation (R) or semi-concrete (S) presentation of the numbers or concepts, typically done through drawings or pictures. Once students understand the concepts currently being worked using visual representations they move toward abstract (A) presentations of the problem using mathematical symbols and numbers. To implement this strategy at home you can use regular household items as manipulatives, for example dried pasta noodles, buttons, pompoms for counting, cardboard shapes or paper plates to use for fractions, tape measure, homemade 100 number chart, number line, different size and color buttons or different pasta shapes for patterns or sorting, craft or popsicle sticks for ones, tens, and 100s etc. and chalk on a sidewalk or driveway or simply copy or art paper and pencil (colored pencils, crayons, etc.). A search on the internet for *household items to use for mathematics* will list a number of links for ideas to use at home to help your child understand mathematics in a concrete or visual representative or semi-concrete way before working things out more abstractly. While recommending that you test strategies out together, please note that both the National Council for Teachers of Mathematics and the Council for Exceptional Children recommend using the CRA/CSA approach to build conceptual understanding. As your child moves from concrete materials to semi-concrete or representational diagrams/drawings, help them to make connections between what they can manipulate in their hands and what they see in a diagram or visual representation of the problem.

Subtraction Strategy—Compensating Strategy

In this strategy students look for ways that they can make challenging or complex numbers simple. For example, 474 – 237 = _____. A way to make either number less complex might be to make 237 be 240, which means you added 3 to the number. If you add 3 to 237 you need to **compensate** by adding 3 to the other number so now 474 becomes 477. My new math problem is 477 – 240 = ___ which is much easier to subtract. You can use a number line to help you show your child how the numbers are moving either up or down based on how you are compensating your original values.

PEMDAS Strategy

This strategy you may well remember yourself from school. When solving a mathematical problem we solve in the order of operations starting with values in parentheses and ending with the subtraction operation outside of the parentheses if present.

Parentheses (a + b − c) =
Exponents b^3 =
Multiplication 2 × 3, 2 * 3 =
Division 42 ÷ 6 =
Addition 8 + 2 =
Subtraction 17 − 5 =

Multiplication Strategy for Sixs, Sevens, Eights and Nines, and Tens
The multiplication strategy for sixs through nines works by bending or folding the finger over. Here are some examples on how to use this strategy.

The multiplication strategy for the nines works where you fold the finger down that you are multiplying by; for example, in 2 × 9 you fold over the finger numbered 2. Look to the left and ask how many fingers are up. This is your tens. The answer would be 1 and then count from the folded finger to the right. The answer would be 8. This number is in the ones place 2 × 9 = 18

Let's try that again. Let's solve 6 × 9. Fold the sixth finger. Count the fingers to the left of the folded finger (tens) equals 5, and count the fingers to right of the folded finger (ones) which equals 4. 5 tens 4 ones equals 54.

For multiplication of 6 through 8 we are going to use the finger strategy a little differently. For the first number (multipli-

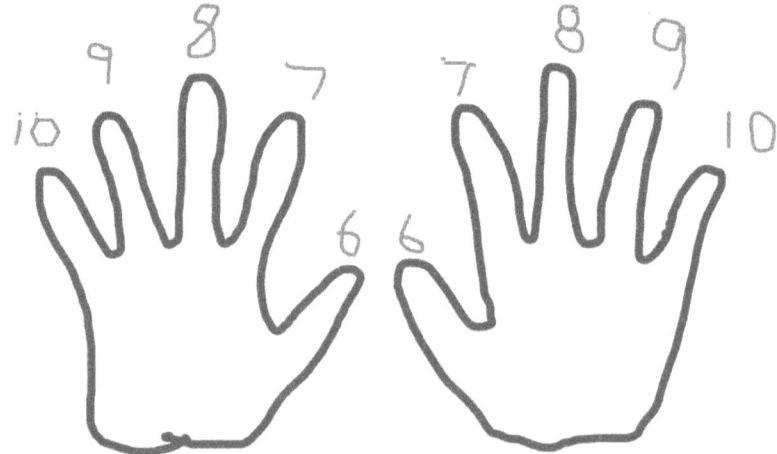

FIGURE 4.1 Multiplication Finger Strategy for Sixs through Nines

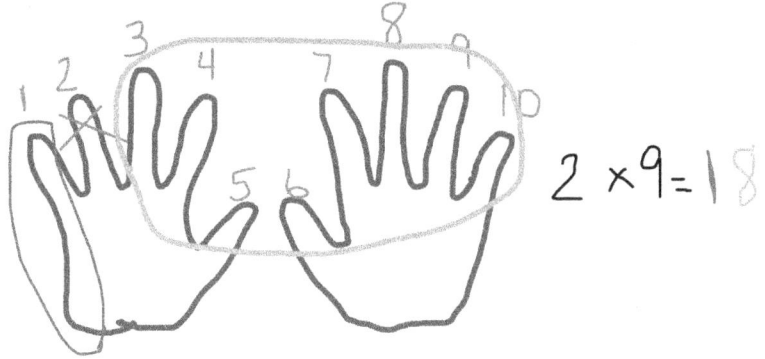

FIGURE 4.2 Multiplication Finger Strategy Example 1

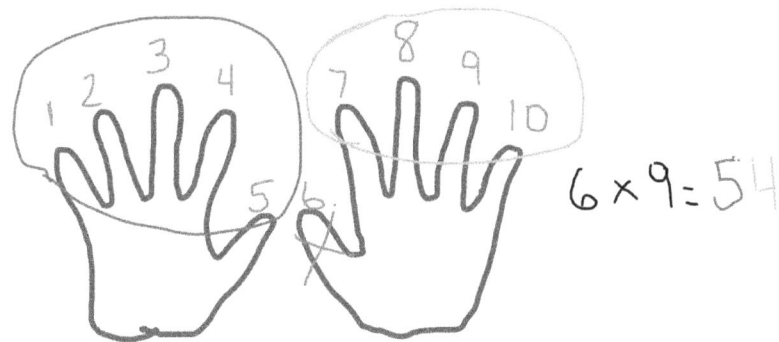

FIGURE 4.3 Multiplication Finger Strategy Example 2

cand) we will use the left hand, and for the number being multiplied by (multiplier) we will use the right hand. You will touch the multiplicand finger and multiplier finger together and add the total number of fingers under the two touching for the tens place. Then you will multiply the number of fingers above the multiplicand with the number of fingers above the multiplier to get your value in the ones place.

The Butterfly Method
The Butterfly Method is used to help students visually see the process to cross-multiply when adding or subtracting fractions with different denominators. First students multiply the top wing on the upper left number (numerator) and the bottom

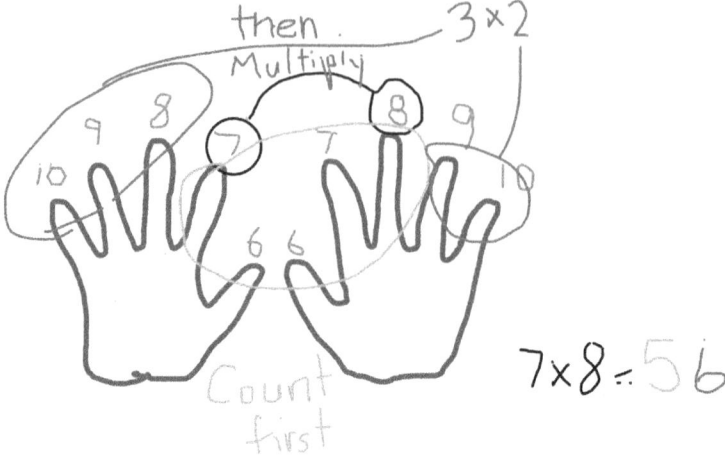

FIGURE 4.4 Multiplication Finger Strategy Example 3

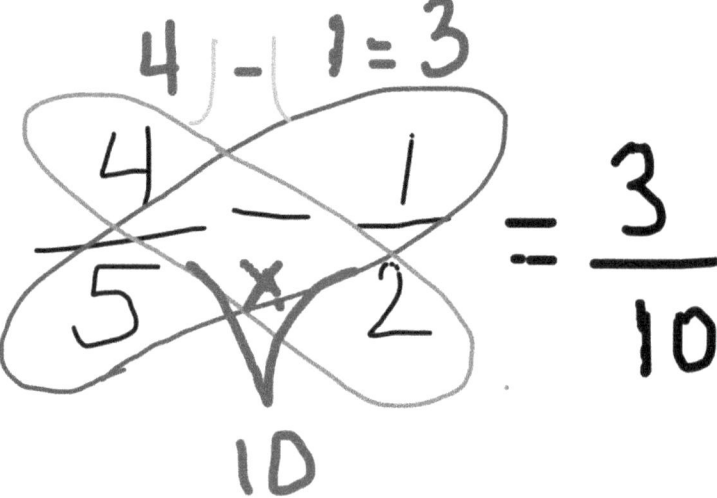

FIGURE 4.5 Examples of the Butterfly Method

wing on the right (denominator) of the butterfly to get the top left number (numerator) and then they multiply the top wing on the upper right and the bottom wing on the left of the butterfly to get the top right number. Next students multiply the two bottom numbers together (denominators).

Story and Word Problem Solving Strategies

Story or word problems require students to read and understand the text, identify and separate relevant information from irrelevant information, represent the problem correctly, identify a strategy to use to solve the problem, computational procedures, and the ability to check their answer to ensure it makes sense (Stevens & Powell, 2016; Jitendra et al., 2013). To work through story or word problems there are several strategies using mnemonic instruction. LDonline shares that mnemonics are proven effective with students of all abilities, but particularly helpful for students with disabilities. Mnemonic instruction strategies guide students by breaking down the steps to understand, analyze, and solve a word or story problem. Teaching students to identify different types of word problems will promote their ability to implement a strategy (Jitendra et al., 2007). One mnemonic to guide the process on identifying the type of problem is to use the strategy **FOPS**.

F—Find problem type
O—Organize using a visual diagram or equation
P—Plan to solve the problem
S—Solve problem

Once the type of problem is identified, your child can implement a strategy to solve the problem. There are several different mnemonics for problem solving. Find the one that makes sense to your child and support them in using it. Here are some more suggestions.

RIDE (Mercer, Mercer, and Pullen,)

R—Read the problem carefully
I—Identify the relevant information
D—Determine the operations and unit for expressing the answer
E—Enter the correct numbers and calculate and check the answer

SIGNS
- S—Survey the question
- I—Identify key words and labels
- G—Graphically draw the problem
- N—Note operation(s) needed
- S—Solve and check problem

STAR (Hott et al., 2014)
- S—Search the words
- T—Translate the words into an equation in picture form
- A—Answer the problem
- R—Review the problem

SQRQCQ or SQ$_3$R (six-step strategy)
- **Survey**—Skim the problem to get an idea or general understanding.
- **Question**—Ask what the problem is about; what information does it require? Change the wording of the problem into a question, or restate the problem.
- **Read**—Read the problem carefully (read aloud if helpful) to identify important information, facts, relationships, and details needed to solve the problem. Highlight information that is relevant or important.
- **Question**—Ask "What operations need to be performed, with what numbers, and in what order? What is given or known, and what is unknown? What are the units?"
- **Compute (or construct)**—Do the computation to solve the problem, or construct a solution by drawing a diagram, making a table, or setting up and solving an equation.
- **Question**—Ask if the solution seems to be correct and the answer reasonable. "Were the calculations done correctly? Were the facts in the problem used correctly? Does the solution make sense? Are the units correct?"

Another strategy for your child to consider using is one that works using key words and builds metacognition (building awareness and understanding of one's own thinking processes).

TABLE 4.1 Word/Story Problem Strategy Organizer

Word/Story Problem:
Survey: **Question:**   **Read:**   **Question:**   **Compute:**   **Question:**

Read—Read the problem.
Ask—What is the problem asking?
Draw—Draw a picture.
Check—Does my drawing match the problem?
Solve—Solve.

Summary

Learning strategies are effective tools for your child to understand mathematical concepts and strategically find a way to build fluency or attack story or word problems. Finding a strategy that is effective in helping your child learn and that your child will use is a double win. Several strategies using mnemonics are often used in solving word or story problems, helping children to pull out the important information and identify the operation.

Resources

Development and Research of Early Math Education (DREME)1https://familymath.stanford.edu/all-about-family-math/
National Library of Virtual Manipulative http://nlvm.usu.edu/en/nav/vlibrary.html
Strategy instruction: What you need to know from Understood https://www.understood.org/en/articles/what-is-strategy-instruction

References

Bryant, D. P. (2021). *Intensifying mathematics interventions for struggling students*. The Guilford Press.

Codding, R. S., Volpe, R. J., & Poncy, B. C. (2016). *Effective math interventions: A guide to improving whole-number knowledge*. Guilford Publications.

Deshler, D. D., Alley, G. R., Warner, M. M., & Schumaker, J. B. (1981). Instructional practices for promoting skill acquisition and generalization in severely learning disabled adolescents. *Learning Disability Quarterly*, *4*(4), 415–421. https://doi.org/10.2307/1510744

Deshler, D. D., & Schumaker, J. B. (1986). Learning strategies: An instructional alternative for low-achieving adolescents. *Exceptional Children*, *52*(6), 583–590. https://doi.org/10.1177/001440298605200610

Dweck, C. S. (2019). The choice to make a difference. *Perspectives on Psychological Science*, *14*(1), 21–25. https://doi.org/10.1177/1745691618804180

Fong, J. P. J., Sutherland, M., & Nelson, G. (2024). Engaging caregivers of students with disabilities in home math activities. *Teaching Exceptional Children*. https://doi.org/10.1177/00400599241256613

Jitendra, A. K., Peterson-Brown, S., Lein, A. E., Zaslofsky, A. F., Kunkel, A. J., Pyung-Gang, J., & Egan, A. M. (2013). Teaching mathematical problem solving: The quality of evidence for strategy instruction priming the problem structure. *Journal of Learning Disabilities*, *48*(1), 51–72. https://doi.org/10.1177/0022219413487408

Manolitsis, G., Georgiou, G. K., & Tziraki, N. (2013). Examining the effects of home literacy and numeracy environment on early reading and math acquisition. *Early Childhood Research Quarterly*, *28*(4), 692–703. https://doi.org/10.1016/j.ecresq.2013.05.004

Nelson, G., Carter, H., Boedeker, P., Knowles, E., Eames, J., & Buckmiller, C. (2024). The effects of math interventions in informal learning environments: A meta-analysis and quality review. *Review of Educational Research*, *94*(1), 112–152. https://doi.org/10.3102/00346543231156182

Patti, A. L., Rafferty, L. A., Budin, S., & Maheady, L. (2021). The role of high leverage practices in effective inclusive elementary schools. In J. McLeskey, L. Maheady, B. Billingsley, M. T. Brownell, & T. J. Lewis (Eds.), *Handbook of effective inclusive elementary schools* (pp. 181–198). Routledge.

Sheldon, S. B., & Epstein, J. L. (2005). Involvement counts: Family and community partnerships and mathematics achievement. *The Journal of Educational Research*, *98*(4), 196–207. https://doi.org/10.3200/JOER.98.4.196-207

Stevens, E. A., & Powell, S. R. (2016). Unpacking word problems for diverse learners: A guide to using schemas. *Childhood Education*, *92*, 86–91. https://doi.org/10.1080/00094056.2016.1134253

5

Special Math Curriculum

Special Math Curriculum Explained

One mom said to us, "Don't some kids need to learn math the old-fashioned way? That's the way I learned and it made sense." Her sentiment might resonate with you since usually when parents refer to old-fashioned learning, they mean rote learning of calculations and math procedures. While today's math requires both procedures and calculations, it also requires a high degree of thinking and reasoning skills to demonstrate conceptual understanding. This implies your child must know how to solve the math as well as extend the knowledge to other ways to solve the problem such as verbal descriptions, expressions, equations, drawings, and graphs. For example, the first-grade teacher might ask, "What math strategies make a 10?"

The type of math your child's teacher teaches today is largely driven by your state's math standards. Standards are the student-centered expectations from which all curriculum, instruction, and assessments are based. This type of educational jargon makes sense to educators but can be confusing to parents. Let's examine each area individually.

- Curriculum: This refers to how the standards are incorporated into the classroom. The curriculum is the instructional material by which the standards are taught.

- Instruction: This is the teacher's delivery and strategies used to implement the curriculum and the standards.
- Assessment: This provides feedback to teachers, students, and parents on the student's level of mastery of the standards. The standards assessments can be ongoing and administered at multiple points throughout the school year or given as one large test toward the end of the year.

In addition to standards, curriculum, instruction, and assessment, students who struggle to achieve the standards must progress through tiered levels of instruction. You might have heard the terms response-to-intervention or multi-tiered systems of support. These terms describe the process most public schools use and which your child must progress through to receive extra help. These were discussed in detail in Chapter 2.

Response-to-intervention (RtI) or multi-tiered systems of support (MTSS) are important because these processes provide the gateway to your child potentially receiving extra help in a special curriculum or instructional materials. There are three tiers of support which are focused on helping students meet mastery of grade level standards. Your child receives different levels of support at different times based on their needs. The purpose of tiered supports is to use data to help the child achieve proficiency.

Tier one support is the instruction all students receive using the school-wide curriculum. When your child struggles and does not meet math proficiency, they receive tier two support, and if they still don't achieve proficiency, they receive tier three support. Tiers two and three are where specialized math curriculum might be introduced. The teacher delivers tier two instruction that is systematic, explicit, and within a small group. The instruction within tier three includes the aforementioned as well as additional instructional time in a smaller group or possibly one-to-one instruction. Tier three can also include the teacher using a specialized math curriculum. Let's examine some of the specialized math curricula.

TouchMath

This is a multisensory approach to teaching mathematics, primarily designed for students with learning disabilities, but it can be used with learners of all abilities. It uses tactile and visual cues to help students understand math concepts, focusing on addition, subtraction, multiplication, and division.

The core principle of TouchMath is that numbers are represented by "touchpoints," which are small dots placed on numbers (for example, a number 2 has two dots, number 4 has four dots, etc.). Students physically touch each point while counting, which helps them associate the number with a physical action. This multisensory approach uses tactile, visual, and auditory learning to engage different senses. This hands-on approach makes it easier for many students to grasp mathematical concepts. TouchMath reinforces learned math concepts through repetition and hands-on interaction.

On Cloud 9 Math

On Cloud 9 Math emphasizes building a solid foundation in basic math skills. According to the publisher's website,

> The On Cloud 9 program develops concept and symbol imagery for math and integrates them with language. These sensory-cognitive functions underlie mathematical reasoning and computation. Unlike programs that only rely on manipulatives, On Cloud 9 transitions to imagery and language to concretize mathematical concepts.

It incorporates a combination of games, activities, and visual aids designed to help students understand key math concepts. The goal of On Cloud 9 Math is to make math enjoyable while encouraging students to develop problem solving skills and number sense.

Math-U-See

Math-U-See is a comprehensive, 13-level hands-on math curriculum designed for students from kindergarten through high school calculus. It's structured to help students understand math concepts in a visual and tactile way, focusing on mastery of one concept before moving on to the next. The program uses manipulatives to illustrate math principles, making abstract concepts more concrete and easier to understand.

Math-U-See takes a step-by-step approach, where students start by learning basic arithmetic and gradually progress to more complex topics like algebra, geometry, and calculus. It allows for a flexible pace and emphasizes mastery. It has a well-defined, structured approach to teaching math, particularly for students who benefit from visuals and hands-on learning.

Jump Math

JUMP Math (Junior Undiscovered Math Prodigies) is a research-based math program designed to help students of all abilities build strong math skills. The program is focused on developing a deep understanding of mathematical concepts through a step-by-step, structured approach. JUMP Math emphasizes the idea that anyone can be successful in math with the right teaching and support. Key features of JUMP math include incremental learning, teacher-led instruction, focus on understanding and not just memorizing procedures, and active engagement. Overall, JUMP Math is a structured, supportive approach to math that helps students build a solid understanding.

Facts on Fire Math

Facts on Fire is a school-wide math program designed to help students quickly and efficiently learn basic math facts including addition, subtraction, multiplication, and division. It uses a variety of activities, drills, and games to reinforce math facts, helping students develop fluency and confidence in their math skills.

The name "Facts on Fire" refers to the idea of igniting or speeding up a student's ability to recall math facts quickly and accurately, as if they were "on fire" with their skills. Key features of Facts on Fire include repetition and practice, games and interactive activities, visual and auditory cues, and progress tracking. Facts on Fire is to help students internalize math facts, making them automatic in their recall. This is crucial for more advanced math work, as fluency with basic facts allows students to focus on problem solving and higher-level math concepts.

Math Made Real

Math Made Real is an educational approach designed to help students understand and apply math concepts in real-life contexts. The program emphasizes practical, hands-on learning that connects abstract math principles to everyday situations, helping students see the relevance and importance of math beyond the classroom. The key features of Math Made Real include real-life application, problem solving focus, hands on learning, and a focus on understanding underlying concepts rather than only memorizing. Math Made Real aims to connect math to the real world and make math less abstract for students.

Times Tales and **My Multiplication Magic** are two additional approaches specifically for students having difficulty with learning and retaining their multiplication facts. Times Tales puts learning multiplication facts into a relatable story so that it makes memorizing multiplication facts more meaningful and memorable. It is a print program. My Multiplication Magic is a multisensory approach to learning math facts. It includes teacher lesson plans, teaching videos, games, worksheets, strategies, and visual prompts. This program is a combination of print and computer-based learning.

What the Research Reports

There is limited research on specific specialized math curricula, but research exists on why students struggle and on characteristics of effective math instruction for students with disabilities. Daly and colleagues (1997) identified five common reasons why students perform academic work poorly, which were, "(a) they do not want to do it, (b) they have not spent enough time doing it, (c) they have not had enough help to do it, (d) they have not had to do it that way before, or (e) it is too hard" (p. 556). When teachers can identify a student's reason for math struggles, they can provide different forms of support that the student might need. In terms of a child with dyscalculia, they will have a combination of reasons for their struggle.

For quite some time, researchers have identified global qualities of effective math instruction for students with disabilities (Burns et al., 2010; Gersten et al., 2009; Miller & Hudson, 2007; Poncy et al., 2007; Powell et al., 2023). Steedly et al. (2008) reported four general approaches for improving math instruction in students. First, teachers must provide systematic and explicit instruction in which students are taught in a defined instructional sequence. Second, self-instruction where students use specific prompting to manage their learning. Third, peer tutoring by pairing students to learn or practice specific math. Fourth, visual representation using manipulatives, pictures, number lines, and graphs. Kong and colleagues (2021) conducted a meta-analysis of effective math word problem interventions and reported consistent evidence in which students with learning disabilities benefited from peer interactions and explicit instruction.

Evidence-based math intervention practices for elementary-age students are described in the What Works Clearinghouse guide (Fuchs et al., 2021). The authors describe six instructional approaches with a strong evidence base for the teaching and learning of math: (a) systematic instruction; (b) focus on the language of math; (c) use multiple representations; (d) use number lines; (e) build fluency; and (f) provide word problem instruction. The first approach, providing systematic instruction is the "set of instructional features that form the backbone of effective systematic instruction" (p. 5). Thus, the while the curriculum is important, it is equally important to teach students in a way which is so clear and precise that it makes learning a straightforward process. In other words, the guesswork is removed so students receive exact steps by instruction.

Teaching students the language of math helps students' understanding of the math they are learning. Teachers should use student-friendly definitions and link vocabulary to concrete representations. When teachers use multiple representations, they are using concrete representations such as physical materials that can be manipulated. Semi-concrete math representations are pictures, graphs, drawings, tables, and number lines, and abstract representations are numbers, equations, and symbols.

Using a number line in math helps students learn concepts and procedures. For example, in early elementary grades number lines are used to teach whole numbers, while in upper elementary grades they are used to teach fractions and decimals. Effective word problem instruction includes teaching students various word problem types, how to identify relevant information in a word problem, and teach word problem vocabulary and language. By teaching students timed math fluency retrieval, it helps students build automatic retrieval which frees up mental energy for understanding. It's also a building block to computing new higher-level math.

Crawford and Snider (2000) studied the effectiveness of math curricula on fourth-grade students' math performance. Teacher A used a direct instruction program and Teacher B used the traditional math basal textbook. Results showed the first year Teacher A's students scored higher on a national achievement test and on a multiplication facts test. During the second year of the study Teacher B also used the direct instruction curriculum, and the students' scores were significantly higher than the previous year. They concluded, "The data from the second year provide evidence that curriculum is a critical factor in student achievement" (p. 141). The researchers also noted that a teacher's skill, dedication, and compassion are important as well.

JUMP Math (Junior Undiscovered Math Prodigies) had independent research showing its effectiveness (Eivers et al., 2014; Garforth, 2013; Randhawa, 2020; Won, 2014). Randhawa (2020) reported this program has increased students' math confidence and "The results from the caregiver surveys illustrate JUMP Math's positive impact on math confidence and reducing math anxiety among the participating children" (p.10). Solomon et al. (2019) reported students taught with JUMP Math made significantly greater progress in computation than their non-JUMP peers. Craig (2019) studied students with learning disabilities and reported 89 percent of students made gains using JUMP

Math and concluded, "This program helps to boost confidence and motivation to provide children with learning disabilities a stronger foundation to succeed in mathematics" (p.9).

TouchMath was shown to be effective for a small group of students with autism and multiple disabilities (Fletcher et al., 2010). Their results showed the students performed single digit addition better with TouchMath as compared to using a number line. Additional unpublished research by master's-degree-earning students showed TouchMath improved addition of students with learning disabilities as well as third-grade general education students.

While this chapter reported on select specialized math curricula, it was not exhaustive. One key takeaway point is that even if a special math curriculum is not available to use with your child, a skilled teacher can effectively help your child using the earlier described six instructional approaches with a strong evidence base for the teaching and learning of math.

Quick Start Guide to Using Special Math Curriculum

Once you know it's dyscalculia, getting started is paramount for success. Suggested next steps include the following:

1. Read additional information on the internet about the special math programs.
2. Search for and contact local providers.
3. If local providers do not use the specific math curriculum you would like, ask if they use any others listed earlier or if they are willing to learn the curriculum.
4. If local providers are not available, search for online tutors using the program.
5. Contact your child's school to request a meeting to discuss options for providing instruction using one of these curriculum programs. Ask the school staff to explain how they use the six math instructional approaches.

Summary

Special math curriculum programs include JUMP Math, TouchMath, Math Made Real, Math-U-See, and On Cloud 9 Math. The independent research supporting these programs varies, as does the curriculum availability for use in schools or with tutors. Despite limited availability of many curricula, struggling learners can successfully learn math. A skilled teacher can effectively teach struggling learners by applying the six instructional approaches with a strong evidence base for the teaching and learning of math: (a) systematic instruction; (b) focus on the language of math; (c) use multiple representations; (d) use number lines; (e) build fluency; and (f) provide word problem instruction.

Resources

www.mathusee.com Math U See curriculum.
https://www.structuringinquiry.com This site offers free math teacher trainings.
https://www.mymultiplicationmagic.com Math facts taught in context.
www.timestales.com Multiplication taught within the context of a story.
https://brianponcy.wixsite.com/mind This site hosts Facts on Fire.
https://www.youcubed.org Practical math resources.

References

Burns, M. K., Codding, R. S., Boice, C. H., & Lukito, G. (2010). Meta-analysis of acquisition and fluency math interventions with instructional and frustration level skills: Evidence for a skill-by-treatment interaction. *School Psychology Review, 39*(1), 69–83.

Craig, R. (2019). *Dyscalculia and building resilience: An evaluation of JUMP Math*. Learning Disabilities Association of Niagara Region. https://ldaniagara.org/wp-content/uploads/2020/01/JUMP-Math-Literature-Review-FINAL.pdf

Crawford, D. B., & Snider, V. E. (2000). Effective mathematics instruction: The importance of curriculum. *Education and Treatment of Children*, *23*(2), 122–142. https://doi.org/10.1353/etc.2000.0014

Daly, E. J., Witt, J. C., Martens, B. K., & Dool, E. J. (1997). A model for conducting a functional analysis of academic performance problems. *School Psychology Review*, *26*(4), 554–574.

Eivers, E., Delaney, E., & Close, S. (2014). *An evaluation of a JUMP Math pilot programme in Ireland*. Educational Research Centre. https://doras.dcu.ie/29881/1/JUMPreport_no_appendices.pdf

Fletcher, D., Boon, R. T., & Cihak, D. F. (2010). Effects of the TOUCHMATH program compared to a number line strategy to teach addition facts to middle school students with moderate intellectual disabilities. In *Education and training in autism and developmental disabilities* (Vol. 45, pp. 449–458). Division on Autism and Developmental Disabilities.

Fuchs, L. S., Newman-Gonchar, R., Schumacher, R., Dougherty, B., Bucka, N., Karp, K. S., Woodward, J., Clarke, B., Jordan, N. C., Gersten, R., Jayanthi, M., Keating, B., & Morgan, S. (2021). *Assisting students struggling with mathematics: Intervention in the elementary grades* (WWC 2021006). Institute of Education Sciences, U.S. Department of Education.

Garforth, K. C. (2013). *JUMP Math in grade four classrooms* (Doctoral dissertation, University of British Columbia).

Gersten, R., Beckmann, S., Clarke, B., Foegen, A., Marsh, L., Star, J. R., & Witzel, B. (2009). *Assisting students struggling with mathematics: Response to intervention (RtI) for elementary and middle schools*. IES National Center for Education Evaluation Practice Guide.

Kong, J. E., Yan, C., Serceki, A., & Swanson, H. L. (2021). Word-problem-solving interventions for elementary students with learning disabilities: A selective meta-analysis of the literature. *Learning Disability Quarterly*, *44*(4), 248–260.

Miller, S. P., & Hudson, P. J. (2007). Using evidence–based practices to build mathematics competence related to conceptual, procedural, and declarative knowledge. *Learning Disabilities Research & Practice*, *22*(1), 47–57.

Poncy, B. C., Skinner, C. H., & Jaspers, K. E. (2007). Evaluating and comparing interventions designed to enhance math fact accuracy and fluency: Cover, copy, and compare versus taped problems. *Journal of Behavioral Education*, *16*, 27–37.

Powell, S. R., Bouck, E. C., Sutherland, M., Clarke, B., Arsenault, T. L., & Freeman-Green, S. (2023). Essential components of math instruction. *Teaching Exceptional Children*, *56*(1), 14–24.

Randhawa, J. (2020). *Bridging the gap to math performance and confidence among students with learning disabilities: A qualitative analysis of the JUMP Math after-school tutoring program.* Learning Disabilities Association of Niagara Region. https://ldaniagara.org/wp-content/uploads/2020/05/JUMP-Math-Report-Final.pdf

Solomon, T., Dupuis, A., O'Hara, A., Hockenberry, M. N., Lam, J., Goco, G., Ferguson, B., & Tannock, R. (2019). A cluster-randomized controlled trial of the effectiveness of the JUMP Math program for improving elementary math achievement. *PLoS ONE*, *14*(10), e0223049. https://doi.org/10.1371/journal.pone.0223049

Steedly, K., Dragoo, K., Arafeh, S., & Luke, S. D. (2008). *Effective mathematics instruction. Evidence for education* (Volume III, Issue I). National Dissemination Center for Children with Disabilities.

Won, D. W. (2014). JUMPing math. *Transit: The LaGuardia Journal on Teaching and Learning Preprints and Works-in-Progress*, *6*, 39–45.

6

Strategies for Making Math Fun

Making Math Fun Explained

Consider all the ways that you have worked with your child on their math. Has it been answering homework questions, helping them with incomplete work, drilling them on their facts, or forcing them to sit down at the computer to prepare for state-required benchmark assessments? These activities are necessary ways to help your child with their math, but often they can lead to tears and frustration. Finding ways to make practicing math competencies more enjoyable can reduce anxiety and demonstrates to your child that you enjoy learning with them.

Do you play Wordle, Sudoku, Connections, or do crossword puzzles on your phone, computer, newspaper, or in a puzzle book? While playing these or any other games, do you realize you are learning while having fun? Fun ways of learning are always more engaging than simply reading about it or doing a worksheet. Math becomes more fun when manipulatives are used to first introduce a concept but also in playing games, reading books that have mathematics connections, solving math riddles, integrating music, and real-world opportunities.

As a parent you have most likely read to your child from the time they were an infant or at the very least a toddler. We know that reading to our children promotes literacy, and we hope for them a love of lifelong reading. Finding books that explore math concepts such as numbers (*Numbers 1 2 3 Everywhere* by Elliot Kaufman), counting (*10 Black Dots* by Donald Crews), fractions (*The Milk Chocolate Fractions Book* by Jerry Pallota and Bob Bolster), etc. can build toward a love of literacy and math. Depending on the age of your child, you can move from reading the story to talking about the concept to connecting it to real life activities such as counting fruit snacks to sharing half a cookie with them to using coins in a vending machine.

When our children are infants we often sing lullabies to help them to become calm and perhaps doze off to sleep. We may stop singing songs to children at home once they start preschool, but song is very much a part of a preschooler's day and even beyond, in elementary school. Children learn songs in school for cleaning up their area, days of the week, how they are feeling, greeting one another, and even related to content. Children will often sing the songs they learn at school to themselves. Just think of the alphabet song, or perhaps you even remember the "Apples & Bananas" song. Songs such as "The Ants Go Marching" and rhymes put to songs such as "One Two Buckle My Shoe" are also something that can be sung in the car and at home, but you can also learn the songs children are singing from school. Singing to or with children definitely doesn't need to stop once they are off to school.

Long before the age of computers, family entertainment and learning came from board games, picture and wooden puzzles, card games, and outdoor play. Chess, checkers, crazy eights, hopscotch, jacks, kickball, or baseball include score keeping, counting, number recognition, and computation. Many of these skills are challenging for children with dyscalculia, and playing them at home reinforces skills as well as provides time together as a family.

What the Research Reports

Research confirms that children's home environment and their parents' expectations, aspirations, and beliefs can greatly affect their attitudes toward mathematics and level of achievement

(Fan, 2001; Sheldon & Epstein, 2005). Providing families ways to get involved in learning math that is fun and easy to do at home can be beneficial for both attitude and academic achievement in math.

Children's Literature

While listening to a bedtime story, children are learning without realizing it. They are learning what fluent reading sounds like when hearing something read smoothly and with expression. They are learning new vocabulary words used in context, and they are comprehending the story while listening to it be read. Playing mathematical games can have a similar effect. Research shows our brains are "wired for pleasure" (Noonoo, 2019). Making math enjoyable by making math fun means children can learn math that doesn't feel like completing another worksheet or answering questions from their textbook. Fun math learning can be experienced through books, music/song, puzzles, games, and real-world experiences.

Arts integration in science, technology, engineering and mathematics has enriched STEM education into what is known as STEAM. The arts in STEM can bring about creativity and innovation. The arts in STEAM can be literature, drama, dance, music, design, visual arts, and even forms of media. Two forms of art that we will connect to in this chapter are literature and music or song. Several mathematics curricula include children's picture story books that connect to each unit standard and are designed to be read at the start of the unit for kindergarten and first grade. The use of colorful illustrations, simple words, and easy-to-discuss scenes in children's picture book literature provide the visual simulation the promotes engagement and learning of young children (Zhang et al., 2023).

Picture books containing math concepts help children see that math is a part of life for everyone (Onesti et al., 2022). Shared reading also engages children in opportunities to use and clarify their understanding of the mathematics vocabulary through conversations (math discourse) about what they are seeing and hearing, further supporting their mathematics conceptual understanding (Purpura & Reid, 2016; Chan et al., 2022). The focus on early literacy skills in preschool classrooms often means fewer introductions of early mathematical concepts for young children. Coelho et al. (2021) discovered that in 168 preschool classrooms, an average of 6 percent of activities focused on math, while the average for literacy activities was 15 percent. This deficit of opportunities to experience mathematics in early childhood classrooms can set the stage for developing a mathematical gap in children who may have math difficulties in their future, especially for children not exposed to mathematical concepts through parental involvement in their environment by counting objects, naming shapes, and making patterns through play.

Picture books can promote early mathematical thinking when we are aware enough to deliberately draw attention to and ask questions about the math-related details in a book (Onesti et al., 2022). Through shared reading of picture books, math conversations provide children an opportunity to use and practice the mathematics vocabulary, reinforcing their knowledge and giving them an opportunity to hear or practice using the words in a new context as well potentially extending math concepts beyond the book to creating math problems, describing attributes, determining probability, and perhaps even data analysis (Onesti et al., 2022) using the concepts and images within the book.

Songs

Do you remember the Schoolhouse Rock songs "I'm Just a Bill" or "Conjunction Junction"? Think of a song from a commercial. Have you ever found yourself singing the song later in the day and it is just stuck in your head? How about a song from your youth? If the song were to be played while you are in your car on your way to work, would you recall the lyrics and be able to sing along decades later? Most people would indicate they could at least remember the chorus and some of the lyrics from listening to the instrumental portion. Did you ever learn a song in your own K–12 school years about a historical event and you can remember parts of it today?

Songs are another way to make math concepts fun and can help children who struggle with math by learning the concepts in a different way. In fact, a NSF grant-funded project that included a study done in college statistics courses found that students indicated that the use of an interactive song (student input) was a good way to engage in learning statistical topics and helped relieve student anxiety about statistical topics, and furthermore student responses on assessments completed post-song showed gains as compared to their assessment pre-song (Lesser et al., 2019). Teachers integrate curriculum through songs and poems to promote learning with procedural memory and can even solicit student participation in writing the songs to help retain the information (Walsh & Coleman, 2023).

RAP, Hip Hop, and POP music beats are more frequently used to engage students at the Middle School grades, while in early childhood and primary grades songs are often sung to tunes such as "Row, Row, Row Your Boat" or "Twinkle, Twinkle, Little Star" and make up a part of the teaching day from welcoming students, to cleaning up centers, to transitioning in the classroom, and even with some content areas (days of the week, alphabet song, planets, money, etc.). Intermediate grades may find themselves somewhere using pop music tunes and rap or even perhaps a cadence march beat. No matter the beat, helping students connect to the math concepts in a way that is relevant and makes real-world connections will help them retain the concepts long after learning them (Walsh & Coleman, 2023).

Games

Mathematical games help students to deepen their mathematical understanding of concepts, reasoning, and applications through providing drill and practical application (Nfon, 2018). Game-based learning (GBL) is described as an environment where game content and game play enhance knowledge and skills acquisition, and where game activities involve problem solving spaces and challenges that provide players/learners with a sense of achievement (Kirriemuir & McFarlane, 2004). In today's world of technology most often we think of game-based learning as games played on a computer or video games, but games can also be in a non-tech or low-tech form.

At school, your child's teacher may use games as a way to reinforce learning mathematical concepts such as Bingo for number recognition, or partnering students together and using a deck of cards to create and solve math facts, or they may even go outside and draw a track with various numbers on it or a hopscotch frame for number recognition and counting. Whether teacher created or commercially produced, board games support number recognition and comprehension, counting, and basic operations (McNelly, 2023).

Many schools also host a family math game night to build student and family sense of belonging and community and involve families in an opportunity to understand the curriculum and how it is being taught. Through teacher modeling, parents learn how to question their child to understand their processes and reasoning as they solve problems, as well as learn how to assist their child when they are struggling. Aside from being a community event, family game nights enable parents to learn skills needed to support their child at home through the continuation of family game night, and children learn to build procedural and conceptual understanding, develop number sense, practice fact fluency, and gain confidence in mathematics (Kessinger, 2014). Recognizing this, Rutherford (2015) suggests that teachers provide repeated opportunities for students to play games, letting mathematical ideas emerge as students notice new patterns, relationships, and strategies. Furthermore, games encourage strategic mathematical thinking as students find different strategies for solving problems and deepen their understanding of numbers; support students' development of computational fluency when played repeatedly; present opportunities for practice; have the potential to allow students to develop familiarity with the number system and with "benchmark numbers" (such as 10s, 100s, and 1000s) while building a deeper understanding of operations; and support a school-to-home connection so parents can learn about their children's mathematical thinking by playing games with them at home (Rutherford, 2015). Whether traditional board games or home-created, hopscotch, or a deck of cards, the use of games can build skills, and you can support your child at home at a pace that works best.

Quick Start Guide to Using Fun Math Learning Activities

Read Together
To make math fun, consider reading picture book literature with your children and discuss concepts of more than, less than, ordinal numbers (first, second, last); patterns, how many, one to one correspondence, fractions, etc. As with all books, any inaccuracies should be pointed out and discussed.

Avoid assumptions of what your child can and cannot do. This recommendation comes from a study where parents assumed their child could eventually count a smaller group of objects (2) and counted the objects that had larger amounts (6, 10) (Goldstein et al., 2016). Assumptions reduce a child's opportunity to practice.

Onesti et al. (2022) make some recommendations of things to look for when considering a book to read with children while making math connections:

Counting Books
Be intentional about helping a child develop the counting sequence by demonstrating how to count a set and learn what each number word means. Scaffolding may be needed for some children by modeling how to count if a child's counting skills are still emerging. Examine counting books to determine how the numbers appear. Are they in a sequential ascending order, out of order, or backwards? Do the objects and numbers accurately and clearly align? Are the objects to be counted arranged linearly (making them easier to count), or do they overlap or appear scattered across a page (making them harder to keep track of)? Do the illustrations allow children to find all of the items to be counted and to keep track of what has already been counted? If illustrations are too abstract or the objects shown in them are close together and difficult to count, using concrete materials to count alongside the story is recommended.

Shape Books
Present opportunities to label shapes but also to discuss geometry principles by exploring their properties, parts, sizes, and

orientations. Discuss the number of sides and corners a shape has, noticing which sides are long and which sides are short. Discuss how some shapes look different even when they have the same defining features, such as when comparing a skinny, long triangle with a short, wide triangle. Point out similarities and differences among shapes, and even rotate a book to explore whether a shape changes or remains the same.

When choosing shape books to read with children look for books that highlight a variety of shapes in various sizes and orientations. Do the books include illustrations and text that accurately demonstrate math, and do these illustrations and text appear in a clear manner that is not distracting or confusing? Do the text, math, and pictures align? For example, if the text states, "Shawn traveled very far to get to his grandma's house," yet the illustration shows Shawn walking from a car in a driveway to the door of a house, children may inaccurately interpret the spatial term far. If you notice incorrect or potentially confusing examples, can you address them? For example, in the instance earlier, a teacher could say: "Here Shawn is just walking up from the car to his grandma's house, but before he got out of the car, he and his father drove all the way from another city! It took them all day to drive to his grandma's house." If a counting book features the numeral 5 next to a picture of six balls (one large and five small), count the six balls. Then specify that 5 is the number of small balls, and recount those. Do the books promote the idea that math is for everyone? A teacher's collection of books should feature a diverse array of characters from different races, genders, cultures, and countries as well as nontraditional families and children with disabilities.

While reading the book with your child, talk about the math on the pages. For example, looking at the image in Figure 6.1, some questions you could ask could be: How many bears are there? Which is larger? Which is smaller? Which bear might weigh more? Why do you think the ____ one might weigh more? Can you make an addition (subtraction) sentence about the bears on these pages?

Any picture book can be used to engage children in math conversations even when math is not the primary focus of the

FIGURE 6.1 Bears

story. Children can draw on their knowledge of size relations when comparing the size of two objects in a book, examining what order the pictures are placed on a page, or how many of various objects are in a picture or on each page throughout a book.

One great thing about books is that they can be read repeatedly as children gain more math knowledge. A book used to help a child understand how to count can be used to practice counting skills when children are ready. Gradually more complex math concepts (such as addition, measurement, or data analysis) can be pointed out as children ask new questions or show an understanding of the concepts discussed when read to them previously.

Sing Together

Songs that children learn during the school day to help with understanding various concepts usually come home in the form of being sung by them. If your child sings a concept learning song from school, ask their teacher for a copy of the song lyrics so that you can support their practice at home and reinforce concepts.

Decades ago children learned multiplication facts from songs on Schoolhouse Rock videos or the Rock or Rock N Learn CD. Today's music is streamed through Pandora, Spotify, or YouTube Music. When traveling anywhere or working with your child in your home on various math concepts you can stream math songs and sing along with your child. A simple search of "math songs" or "math songs for kids" pulls a plethora of different artists and math concepts from counting and addition to pi and the quadratic formula, either for free or for a small fee.

Play Games Together

Simply play games with your child and enjoy! Children enjoy spending time with family members. Playing board games and card games is a built-in way to spend time together, have fun, and learn. Some games are about math by the way they are designed to be played. Yahtzee (number combinations and multiples), Uno (number recognition), Candyland or Chutes and Ladders (counting spaces), Blokus (shapes), Dominoes (counting), The Game of Life (money) and Monopoly (purchasing, making change, and selling) are ready to go, and the very act of playing them engages them in math. Even a deck of cards solicits math concepts such as number recognition and sequencing through a variety of card games and, at a more challenging level, using strategic thinking to identify which cards will go into the CRIB while adding, counting by fives, and making different combinations as you move your peg around the board in Cribbage. A deck of cards can be used to practice math facts by adding two number cards, subtracting one card from another, or multiplying two cards. Checkers, chess, tic-tac-toe, and Battleship can teach probability and strategic problem solving. Board and card games are great multisensory ways to make learning math fun while at home.

Summary

Parent involvement and support in reviewing math concepts and reinforcing skills is necessary to close the gaps children may have or to build fluency. Extra practice using a boring extra practice worksheet can sometimes feel like a battle of wills leaving both parents and child feeling frustrated and disappointed in the way their time was spent together. Making mathematics fun using games can help switch everyone's mindset from being too hard or too boring to engaging and exciting when there is a chance at winning. Songs also make math learning fun, whether a song is sung to an old familiar tune or to the rhythm of the most current pop music song.

If children enjoy the beat and they understand and memorize the lyrics, they can often be seen silently singing the song with their heads bobbing up and down while they are taking a test. Lastly, books are another way to make learning math fun. Books have a way of making math concepts connect to real life and can be used repeatedly to build skills and enrich critical thinking. The storyline and images engage children, and when read together with a parent it means quality time spent together.

Resources

BOOKS

40 Children's Books That Foster a Love of math from the Development and Research in early Mathematics Education (DREME) https://dreme.stanford.edu/news/40-childrens-books-that-foster-a-love-of-math/

The Best Children's Books for Early math Learning from the Erickson Institute Early math Collaborative https://earlymath.erikson.edu/the-best-childrens-books-for-early-math-learning/

12 Books to Excite Your Child's Mathematical Imagination from PBS https://www.pbs.org/parents/thrive/12-books-to-excite-your-childs-mathematical-imagination

SONGS

Jack Hartmann Kids Music Channel on YouTube https://www.youtube.com/channel/UCVcQH8A634mauPrGbWs7QlQ

Patty Skukla Kids TV-Children's Songs available on YouTube https://www.youtube.com/@pattyshukla and Spotify Channel https://open.spotify.com/artist/6lQcPZtrhQfbSkXafngUYc?si=85bea463ec5a41a4&nd=1&dlsi=9e502b05e38c4728

Math Songs by NUMBEROCK available on YouTube https://www.youtube.com/@NUMBEROCKLLC

The Pi Song (100 Digits of Pi) on Spotify https://open.spotify.com/track/29tudnbTiGFQFcAemVIXlz

Quadratic Formula Song on Spotify https://open.spotify.com/track/58wC7hkQ7qoyXkZh3Rivkm

GAMES

The Big List of board Games that Inspire Mathematical Thinking from Mind Education https://www.mindresearch.org/resources/the-big-list-of-board-games-that-inspire-mathematical-thinking/

Building Fluency through Games (Grades K-5) from EMBARC.Online https://embarc.online/mod/page/view.php?id=8086

Eureka Math™ Card Games https://embarc.online/pluginfile.php/31794/mod_page/content/3/card_games-en.pdf

References

Chan, J. Y. C., Sera, M. D., & Mazzocco, M. M. (2022). Relational language influences young children's number relation skills. *Child Development*, *93*(4), 956–972. https://doi.org/10.1111/cdev.13737.

Coelho, V., Åström, F., Nesbitt, K., Sjöman, M., Farran, D., Björck-Åkesson, E., Christopher, C., Granlund, M., Almqvist, L., Grande, C., & Pinto, A. I. (2021). Preschool practices in Sweden, Portugal, and the United States. *Early Childhood Research Quarterly*, *55*, 79–96.

Fan, X. (2001). Parental involvement and students' academic achievement: A growth modeling analysis. *The Journal of Experimental Education*, *70*(1), 27–61. www.jstor.org/stable/20152664

Goldstein, A., Cole, T., & Cordes, S. (2016). How parents read counting books and non-numerical books to their preverbal infants: An observational study. *Frontiers in Psychology*, *7*, 1100. https://doi.org/10.3389/fpsyg.2016.01100

Kessinger, S. (2014). Family game nights. *Teaching Children Mathematics*, *21*(3), 146–152. https://www.jstor.org/stable/10.5951/teacchilmath.21.3.0146

Kirriemuir, J., & McFarlane, A. (2004). *Literature review in games and learning* (Report No. 8). NESTA Futurelab. https://www.nestafuturelab.org

Lesser, L. M., Pearl, D. K., Weber III, J. J., Dousa, D. M., Carey, R. P., & Haddad, S. A. (2019). Developing interactive educational songs for introductory statistics. *Journal of Statistics Education*, *27*(3), 238–252. https://doi.org/10.1080/10691898.2019.165506

McNelly, N. (2023, October 2). Using board games to teach math to young children. *Edutopia*. https://www.edutopia.org/article/board-games-that-teach-elementary-math/

Nfon, N. F. (2018). The use of mathematical games and secondary school students' achievement in mathematics in Fako Division, South West Region of Cameroon. *Journal of Education & Entrepreneurship*, *5*(1), 21–32.

Noonoo, S. (2019, February 12). Playing games can build 21st century skills. Research explain how. *EdSurge*. https://www.edsurge.com/news/2019-02-12-playing-games-can-build-21st-century-skills-research-explains-how

Onesti, M., Uscianowski, C., & Mazzocco, M. M. (2022). Extending the math in picture books. *YC Young Children*, *77*(3), 42–49. https://www.jstor.org/stable/10.2307/27185938

Purpura, D. J., & Reid, E. E. (2016). Mathematics and language: Individual and group differences in mathematical language skills in young children. *Early Childhood Research Quarterly*, *36*, 259–268.

Rutherford, K. (2015). Why play math games? *Teaching Children Mathematics*. https://www.nctm.org/Publications/TCM-blog/Blog/Why-Play-Math-Games_/

Sheldon, S. B., & Epstein, J. L. (2005). Involvement counts: Family and community partnerships and mathematics. *The Journal of Educational Research*, *98*(4), 196–206. http://www.jstor.org/stable/27548080

Walsh, J., & Coleman, B. (2023). Using music to teach math in middle school. *South Carolina Association for Middle Level Education Journal*, 144–151.

Zhang, Q., Sun, J., & Yeung, W.-Y. (2023). Effects of using picture books in mathematics teaching and learning: A systematic review of 2000–2022. *British Review of Education*. https://doi.org/10.1002/rev3.3383

7

Math Accommodations

Math Accommodations Explained

Federal legislation (Individuals with Disabilities Education Act [IDEA], Americans with Disabilities Act [ADA]) makes it incumbent upon public schools to identify and address barriers that prevent students with disabilities from having fair access to and successful participation in the general education curriculum. If there is a notable gap between what is *expected* of your child and what your child is *able* to do independently, then accommodations via an Individualized Education Plan (IEP) or a 504 plan may be warranted (see Chapter 9—Effective School Plans).

Accommodations are compensatory tools and strategies that can help your child overcome any barriers they may encounter as the result of their learning differences as they progress through their schooling. If you answer "yes" to any of the following questions, then your child may benefit from an individualized accommodation plan:

- ♦ Is your child spending too much time on math at school and/or at home?
- ♦ Is your child getting frustrated during math tasks at school and/or at home?

DOI: 10.4324/9781003586326-8

- Is your child showing signs of anxiety when engaged in math-related demands at school and/or at home?
- Is your child failing or leaving tasks incomplete despite the time spent in both of these environments?

Note that the questions posed here do not pertain to your child's classroom experiences alone. As it is common for children to "act out" where they feel the safest, you may very well be the first to observe the extent to which your child is struggling to keep up and keep it together! As your child's biggest advocate, it is important to be informed about what accommodations your child may be eligible for and how to ask for them. But first, there are some general facts about accommodations that would be helpful to know prior to meeting with your educational team.

There is a difference between accommodations and modifications:

- Accommodations change *how* your child learns, not *what* your child learns. They also can change how your child demonstrates what they know. Accommodations do not alter the curriculum or lower standards or expectations.
  - Examples: allowing the use of a calculator, or extended time for testing
- Modifications, on the other hand, alter learning objectives and/or expectations. Modifications reduce academic demand and rigor.
  - Examples: completing addition tasks rather than multiplication, or taking an alternative standardized assessment

Classroom accommodations are generally provided in four ways:

- Presentation—How information is presented (auditorily, visually, digitally, etc.)
- Responding—How students show what they know/have learned (orally, in writing, etc.)

- Setting—How the environment is adapted (space, noise, lighting, etc.)
- Scheduling—How time demands and schedules are adjusted (e.g., extended time, time of day, etc.)

Standardized testing accommodations are defined at the state and federal level:

- IDEA requires that students with disabilities participate in state or district-wide assessments.
- Students with accommodations must take the same assessment and be held to the same standard and criteria.
- Accommodations permitted during standardized testing should reflect those that are utilized during routine classroom assessments to be justified during standardized assessments.
- Accommodations for standardized testing must be explicitly stated in the students' educational support plans.
- Guidance for accommodating students during standardized assessment is further clarified at the state level (see the resources section of this chapter).

Beware of False Statements or Negative Attitudes About Accommodations

- The goal of accommodations is to "level the playing field," NOT to create an unfair advantage as some may falsely claim!
- Accommodations are student specific, NOT setting or teacher specific!
- Accommodations are designed to address a child's skill deficit (can't do), motivational deficit (won't do), or both (won't do because it is hard). Both are manifestations of the disability and should be treated as such!
- Accommodations are based on the child's best interest, NOT on others' preferences, cost, or convenience!
- Accommodations are selected by a team (including you as the parent), NOT pre-determined by a computer-generated checklist!

- It matters what your child thinks and how they feel about their accommodations!
- Accommodations are designed to increase independence, NOT to enforce compliance!

Best practices in accommodating students with learning disabilities center on individualized supports that enable students to have equitable access to instruction and assessment, while maintaining the same academic rigor and fostering independence. To ensure your child receives the maximum benefit from their potential accommodations, we provide a brief summary of the research describing their value to students with dyscalculia, educators, and yourself.

What the Research Reports

Michaelson (2007) detailed a number of research-supported, yet practical, strategies for accommodating the mathematical cognition of dyscalculic children in inclusive classrooms. Here, the author highlighted the recommendations put forth by Trott in 2003, which have proven effective for this specific population of learners over time. Together, these authors endorse the following:

- Compensate for reading skills: Break up blocks of text, use a sans serif font, avoid justification of text, use colored overlays.
- Compensate for problem solving skills: Photocopy math books and reorder sections in a more logical way, break down multi-step problems, use a line reader, use colored pens to highlight different parts of a question.
- Redesign Instruction: Supplement incomplete notes, post large posters to support recall of basic concepts, use mind-map diagrams, maximize visuals, adjust pacing, teach organization, study/time management skills.

In addition to addressing the known core cognitive deficits, researchers concerned with long-term and equitable outcomes for students with disabilities (post-secondary, employment) emphasize the importance of promoting self-determination skills (the ability to set goals and make informed decisions on one's own behalf) as early as the elementary school years. In 2013, Hart an Brehm published, "A Model for Training Elementary Students to Self-Advocate for IEP Accommodations" in which they describe ten steps teachers can follow to help students with disabilities to become more "self-determined." The Hart and Brehm model outline the following sequential steps:

1. Obtain parent consent
2. Assist students with academic goal setting
3. Introduce accommodations
4. Investigate and model accommodations
5. Help students determine where and when they receive accommodations
6. Help students determine the importance of their accommodations
7. Help students learn how to ask for their accommodations
8. Introduce cue card (scripting how to ask) and engage them in roleplay (to practice)
9. Describe and practice action steps if student is not given the accommodation
10. Monitor student progress and troubleshoot areas of difficulty

The researchers clearly assert that self-advocacy skills (speaking up for oneself, communicating needs and rights to others) are key to improving both the academic achievement and overall quality of life outcomes for students with disabilities. Yet, the authors caution educators from shifting the responsibility of accommodation management to students. Rather, they suggest students be reminded that they are a valued member of the educational team and that it is the role of the teachers and administrators to address concerns related to inconsistent or ineffective implementation of accommodation plans.

In 2025, Flyut and colleagues reported on parents' perspectives about the decision-making process during which reasonable accommodations for their primary-school-aged children with special needs (including but not limited to dyscalculia) were determined. Their findings identified the following overarching concerns about the role of parents:

- Parents, by and large, perceived schools as the primary decision-maker in determining reasonable accommodations.
- Parents expressed a feeling of being suppressed by school stakeholders.
- Parents perceived the decision-making process as vague, ambiguous.

The authors also noted a number of factors that contributed to the more positive experiences reported by parents. Parents who felt more empowered in the process had the following in common: they had their own skills and knowledge; they had adaptive coping styles; they had involved partners; they had a clear communication style; they recognized the potential of their child to succeed. The researchers also call attention to the fact that parents' satisfaction with the process was higher when decision-making procedures and communication with school staff was more transparent and effective.

In order to empower parents and professionals to adopt a more collaborative decision-making process, the authors call for a reconceptualized framework for facilitating discussions between the two groups of stakeholders. The findings of the current study support the larger body of research noting the importance of including all stakeholder perspectives (school professionals, parents, and children with special needs as self-advocates) when refining school processes and making decisions that affect all who are involved. Recognizing the importance of collaborative decision making and parent empowerment, here we highlight best practices for accommodating and supporting your child to help you in your current and/or future discussions (see Chapter 10—Collaborating with Professionals).

Quick Start Guide to Using Math Accommodations

In 2025, Educational clinician Susan Ardila published a parent-friendly guide describing evidence-based accommodations for dyscalculic students across grade levels and categories of support (i.e., instructional, testing, homework, executive functioning, tools/physical aids). This "accommodation bank," from which educators can draw ideas from, illustrates the types of targeted supports that may compensate for the core cognitive deficits that contribute to poor math performance throughout the lifespan (e.g., working memory, processing speed, attention, visual spatial thinking, etc.). Here, we provide you with an adapted list of the author's recommendations categorized by grade level and environment (school and home) (see the reference section of this chapter for more information on the guide).

Grades K–2: Foundations of Numeracy

Classroom Accommodations:

- Use of manipulatives (counters, cubes, etc.)
- Color-coded materials for place value, operation signs, multi-step steps
- Enlarged paper with clear spacing
- Finger-counting visuals
- Number paths and visual-tactile number lines (floor tape, finger tracing)
- Step-by-step verbal directions with modeling
- Use of songs, rhythm, and finger counting for fact development
- Pair visuals with auditory instructions
- Work/break timers (e.g., ten-minute work, five-minute movement)
- Step checklists with simple icons (scaffolding independence)
- Movement-integrated tasks (write the number, then jump it out!)
- Frequent feedback and verbal praise

Testing Accommodations:
- One-on-one or small group assessments
- Allow student to respond orally or through manipulatives
- Flexible response formats (drawings, pointing, matching)
- Instructions and word problems read aloud
- Break into shorter segments
- Extended time/no timed tests

Homework Accommodations:
- Reduce problems per page (three to five max)
- Provide guided examples for homework math centers for skills reinforcement
- Use of visual aids (charts, maps, posters)
- Open-note or take-home quizzes

Grades 3–5: Building on Foundations/Strategic Fluency

Classroom Accommodations:
- Anchor charts for math vocab and operations
- Step-by-step templates for problem solving
- Math strategy notebooks or journals
- Use of visual aids (multiplication charts, fraction strips)
- Daily preview and reteach of math vocabulary with visuals
- Color coding for place value and regrouping steps
- Timed work periods followed by self-check
- Visual "math maps" for multi-step procedures
- Multiplication apps/games for low-pressure fluency
- Dry-erase boards for scratch work, Foldables, flipbooks, or interactive notebooks
- Graph paper, math grid paper

Testing Accommodations:
- Student-created notecard with worked examples
- Access to number lines, visuals, and fraction bars
- Small group setting with extended time

- Give partial credit for correct setup even if computation is incorrect
- Use of manipulatives during assessments (if conceptually appropriate)
- Option to read problems aloud or explain answers orally

Homework Accommodations:
- Option to explain verbally, via video, or typed
- Sentence stems or graphic organizers for math writing
- Highlighted key words in word problems
- Chunking of multi-step problems into guided phases

Grades 6–8: Concrete to Abstract Thinking

Classroom Accommodations:
- Work examples with color-coded steps
- Access to reference cards for formulas and vocabulary
- Interactive notebooks with guided templates
- Metacognitive scaffolds: think-alouds, check-yourself rubrics
- Re-teaching time built into weekly schedule
- Preview of vocabulary and task structure before instruction
- Planner scaffolds (e.g., "What do I need? When is it due?")
- Explicit self-monitoring tools and checklists
- Peer editing or math study buddy system
- Color-coded organizers for solving expressions or equations
- Check-in meetings with teacher
- Graphing software
- Screen readers for word problems

Testing Accommodations:
- Notecard with worked examples, vocabulary, and formulas
- Access to calculator (except where basic computation is the objective)

- Extended time
- Reduced items, with alternate demonstrations
- Use of scratch paper, graph paper, and workspace organizers
- Small group or distraction-reduced room
- Option to respond in writing, audio, or typed format

Homework Accommodations:
- Modified expectations (e.g., choose five out of ten problems)
- Multimodal response options (typed, oral, sketched)
- Homework in smaller chunks with embedded examples
- Project-based assessments instead of timed tests
- Visual scaffolding for equation building

Grades 9–12: Advanced Applications and Independence

Classroom Accommodations:
- Personalized examples in notes (previous tests/homework corrections)
- Flipped lessons or video-based re-teaching
- Access to formulas and solved problems during lessons
- Scaffolded guided notes with visual supports
- Pre-access to complex word problems with time to annotate
- Time management coaching (e.g., Google Calendar, paper planner hybrid)
- Task initiation strategies (e.g., "start with easiest problem")
- Metacognitive tracking (error logs, what went well/what didn't reflections)
- One-on-one check-ins with learning specialist
- Voice-to-text or screen reading for word problems
- Math glossaries, visual study guides

Testing Accommodations:
- Extended time (twice the time standard in some cases)
- Small group testing with calming accommodations

- Notecard (student-created and teacher-approved) with formulas and examples
- Calculator allowed unless computation skill is primary goal
- Use of colored pencils or highlighting to organize multi-step problems
- Pre-approved reference sheets for standardized exams (if allowed)
- Alternative assessment options (project, oral defense, visual models)

Homework Accommodations:
- Project-based learning alternatives
- Option to present math concepts orally or visually
- Reduced problem sets with full-credit options
- Clarified rubrics and exemplars

Although there is no "one-size-fits-all" approach to accommodating dyscalculia, having an understanding of effective and developmentally appropriate supports will help you become an informed advocate who can actively participate in your child's educational programming at all the important ages and stages.

Visual Supports: "A Closer Look"

As evidenced here and in the summarized literature throughout this book, visual supports can be highly beneficial for students with dyscalculia and other learning disabilities. Visual aids (number lines, color-coded materials, written or pictorial checklists, etc.) help to lessen the cognitive load the dyscalculic child experiences when engaged in mathematical thinking. Subsequently, we illustrate a few of the commonly used and easy-to-introduce visual tools from the recommendations provided earlier (see resource list for more examples).

Teaming Up: Advocating for the Right Accommodations

In subsequent chapters we will guide you through the educational process and discuss best practices for working with school

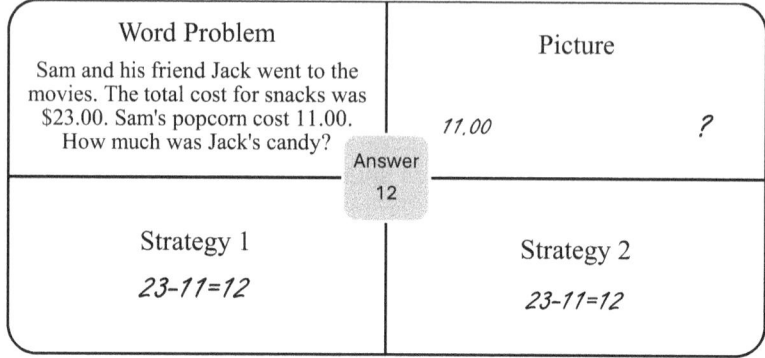

FIGURE 7.1 Example of a Graphic Organizer Used to Support Solving Word Problems

Order of Operations		
P	( )	Parentheses
E	X²	Exponents
M	×	Multiplication
D	÷	Division
A	+	Addition
S	−	Subtraction

FIGURE 7.2 Example of a Mnemonic Device Supporting Correct Order of Operations

My Accommodation Tool Kit

My Classroom Tools:

☑
☑
☑
☑

My Testing Tools

☑
☑
☑

FIGURE 7.3 Example of an Accommodation "At A Glance" Sheet

professionals to ensure you and your child feel well supported and empowered as you progress through this journey together. However, before you take on an advocacy role in your child's school, we would like you to note the following list of dos and don'ts when participating in the decision-making process that determines your child's accommodations.

Do:
- Select accommodations based on individual need
- Do request clarification/justification on selected strategies
- Document all selected accommodations on the IEP or 504 plan
- Reference state assessment policies
- Consult with your child

Don't:
- Take a "kitchen sink" approach
- Copy and paste accommodations from a predetermined list
- Assume accommodations will be upheld that are not in writing
- Introduce accommodations for the first time on testing day
- Ignore child's strengths and preferences

From Plan to Implementation: Bringing Accommodations to Life

Developing a list of student-specific accommodations is only the first step in the intervention process. It is crucial that all team members (including you!) understand why and how each accommodation should be introduced and monitored in "real life."

It is equally important that everyone is aware of what their individual and collective responsibilities are as they transition from plan development to plan implementation. At minimum, all team members should know the who, what, when, where, why, and how of accommodations. Consider the following when discussing accommodations with your child's team:

- **Who** will be in charge of what accommodations (teaching, implementing, monitoring)?
- **What** specific accommodations are needed/no longer needed?
- **When** is each accommodation needed (time of day, tasks)?
- **Where** will each take place (classrooms, home)?
- **Why** is each accommodation needed (what skill or motivational gap is addressed)?
- **How** will each accommodation be introduced/taught to the child?

Report, Revisit, Revise: Monitoring the Effectiveness of Accommodations

Even when team members carefully select accommodations with your child's unique learning profile in mind, it is possible that some intervention choices will be a poor match for your child or their respective learning environments. For this reason, a plan for recording the consistency in which accommodations are used and the extent to which they effectively address your child's deficits is imperative.

Although your child will not outgrow dyscalculia, they are likely to outgrow their accommodations as they progress through the curriculum. Therefore, it is also necessary to consider the age appropriateness and level of complexity of the supports provided at different grade levels. We suggest the use of downloadable or easy-to-create template forms for supporting the consistency of implementation and reporting on accommodations over time. Some commonly used types of templates include the following:

- Quick reference or "at-a-glance guides" with bullet pointed accommodations for classroom and/or testing situations
- Accommodation tracking forms recording when and by whom accommodations have been provided throughout the school day
- A checklist of tools and supplies that the student should have in math class/testing scenarios

♦ Scripts for students to request/advocate for their accommodations

Summary

In this chapter, we provide you with a broad overview of the educational accommodations that your child may be eligible for and benefit from as they progress through the general education curriculum. We offer a detailed list of evidence-based and age-appropriate strategies for accommodating your child's unique learning needs both in school and at home and prepare you to advocate for the most appropriate accommodations at the most appropriate time. We also encourage you to recognize the importance of individualized accommodation plans coupled with a well-thought-out procedure for successful and consistent implementation over time and across settings.

Resources

https://www.parentcenterhub.org/accommodations/—Center for Parent Information and Resources: Supports, Modifications, and Accommodations for Students

https://www.understood.org/en/articles/download-graphic-organizers-to-help-kids-with-math—Understood.com: Download Graphic Organizers to Help with Math

https://nceo.umn.edu/docs/OnlinePubs/NCEOReport437.pdf—National Center for Educational Outcomes: State Requirements

References

Ardila, S. (2025). The complete parent guide to math accommodations for dyscalculia (K 12). *figshare*. https://doi.org/10.6084/m9.figshare.29132237.v1

Hart, J. E., & Brehm, J. (2013). Promoting self-determination: A model for training elementary students to self-advocate for IEP accommodations. *Teaching Exceptional Children*, *45*(5), 40–48. https://doi.org/10.1177/004005991304500505

Michaelson, M. T. (2007). An overview of dyscalculia: Methods for ascertaining and Accommodating dyscalculic children in the classroom. *The Australian Mathematics Teacher*, *63*(3), 17–22.

Trott, C. (2003). Mathematics support for dyslexic students. *MSOR Connections*, *3*(4), 17–20.

8

Math Technology

Math Technology Explained

Mathematics is important to technology, and technology is important to mathematics. Technology does not replace instruction but aids instruction, enhances learning, and reinforces skills. Technology can provide children access to mathematics concepts. During the COVID pandemic, students moved out of the classroom and into their homes, and the need for access to technology held an entirely new meaning. Through various technologies mathematics has become both more accessible and enriching.

We live in a digital world where even ordering and paying for items is processed using technology. Spell checker on your computer, voice to text messaging, and word prediction are tech tools you probably use daily. Artificial intelligence is a daily topic in education. Children as young as 2 may try to swipe their television set to change the channel similarly to the iPad or cellular device they are engaged with. Technology is an everyday part of our lives in our homes and schools. Digital curriculum resources and textbooks have often replaced hardbound textbooks. Instructional curriculum-based materials are developed with learning resources and activities for the classroom Smartboard. Even state-required mathematics benchmark assessments are taken on the computer as opposed to paper and pencil. The

DOI: 10.4324/9781003586326-9

Tier	Description	Example
Substitution	Technology acts as a direct substitute, with no functional change	Video of a lesson on how to compare fractions with different denominators
Augmentation	Technology acts as a direct tool with a functional change	Use a digital number line to compare fractions with different denominators
Modification	Technology allows for a significant task redesign	Use of digital tools to compare fractions with different denominators
Redefinition	Technology allows for creation of new tasks which were inconceivable before now	Use technology to have students compare fractions in different recipes

FIGURE 8.1 SAMR Tiers of Technology

SAMR Model, developed by Ruben Puentedura and presented in Figure 8.1, outlines four tiers of online learning where technology is integrated. The tiers of substitution and augmentation enhance learning, and the tiers modification and redefinition transform learning. The SAMR tiers of technology can be integrated in math learning to provide access to doing math with assistive technology (AT) and in learning math with instructional technology (IT).

The Individuals with Disabilities Education Act Amendments (IDEA) of 2004 defines an assistive technology (AT) device as

> any item, piece of equipment, or product system, whether acquired commercially off-the-shelf, modified, or customized, that is used to increase, maintain or improve the functional capabilities of a child with a disability. The term does not include a medical device that is surgically implanted, or the replacement of such device (SEC 602[1]) (https://sites.ed.gov/idea/statute-chapter-33/subchapter-i/1401).

The AT devices that might be found in a classroom can be electronic (computer, tablets, talking calculators, digital recorder, software programs) and non-electronic (pencil grip, graph paper, magnifying screen). Both electronic/high tech and non-electronic/low tech are useful in supporting students with mathematics difficulties.

What the Research Reports

The National Council of Teachers of Mathematics (NCTM) position on equitable integration of technology for mathematics learning states that

> using the capabilities of technology is essential for educators and learners to inform and transform how they learn, experience, communicate, assess, and do mathematics. Technology should be used to develop and deepen learner understanding, stimulate interest in the mathematics being learned, and increase mathematical proficiency. When technology is used strategically, it provides more equitable access and opportunities for each and every learner to actively engage and participate in the learning of mathematics.
>
> (NCTM, 2023)

Assistive technology (AT) is a collection of resources and tools developed and utilized to assist students with disabilities in overcoming obstacles that interfere with their ability to learn (Abdelwahab et al., 2025). High- and low-tech AT tools can help students who struggle with computing, organizing, and copying math problems. Students that struggle with writing math problems down may benefit from using graph paper, while those who struggle with computing math facts fluently may benefit from using a calculator. Technology and AT assist students who struggle in getting access to curriculum and increase their potential to engage similarly as their peers. Low-tech AT is easy to use and inexpensive. It does not require programming and includes simple, non-electronic aids like magnifiers, pencil-holding devices, large-font simple rules, and graph paper, whereas high-tech AT are more complex, programmable devices like talking calculators, computers, apps (Abdelwahab et al., 2025). Due to high-tech AT's complex structure it is often more expensive and less accessible in most school districts.

A review of the research of the use of assistive technology used by students with disabilities showed that students with visual disabilities most frequently use AT, with students with hearing deficits next, and then non-specific disabilities next. The types of technologies used by these students were high-tech AT in nature, including computers, mobile devices, hardware and software, and internet based (Abdelwahab et al., 2025). While this study examined AT in a general sense across all content, mathematics is often a content area where students could benefit from quality mathematics instruction supported by special education interventions and strategies including the use of AT. Technology-based learning using software is very effective in improving math skills of children with dyscalculia (Kaur et al., 2018). Software can be accessed anytime and anywhere. The repetition of concepts students work on using software can strengthen their skills and memory.

The use of AT when teaching math can improve all students' functioning in their learning environment and reduce the experiences of students with math learning difficulties such as verbalizing problems, estimation, problem solving, and organization (Akpan & Beard, 2014); however assistive technology, whether low or high tech, needs to meet the individual child's needs. A technology tool that is helpful for one student may not be helpful for another, and a tool that is unhelpful goes unused. Selecting the right AT device for any one person requires careful analysis of the specific strengths, experiences, limitations, interests, knowledge of the individual along with the specific tasks needing to be performed (graphing, computations, etc.), the context in which it will need to happen (school, home, work), and the AT device itself (reliability, ease of use, cost, compatibility with other devices, etc.) (Raskind, 2013) while keeping in mind that in addition to math learning there may also be a need to learn how to use the technology.

While technology is promoted by NCTM, it is important to make sure the technology is a match to your child and their needs, as well as being sure the technology being used does not increase their math anxiety. Automaticity of math facts is important; however, high speed frequency computation software programs can produce anxiety (Boaler, 2014) and miss out on the opportunity to support students to think deeply, discover patterns, and make connections to what is happening to numbers when having to complete computations too quickly (Picha, 2018). Similarly to playing games in math, technology can make math fun, so look for tech tools that help make math learning better and bring joy while learning.

Quick Start Guide to Using Assistive Technology

Find Out What AT Is Available

The first step in using AT/IT is to understand what is available and to explore different AT technology tools so determine if they are a match to your child. Talk with your child's teacher to learn what AT tools are being used in your child's school or school district. It is important to understand that not all tools discovered from an internet search or what you may learn from a parent whose child attends school in another school district is available within your child's school district, but it is important to know what is being used (all forms of technology) and what is available within the entire district. Ask how your child engages with the technology. You will want to know if your child will willingly use the tool at home in addition to the school day. Ask to be trained on technology tools that are provided to your child at their school. You will also want to be sure that the technology tool is compatible with other technology your child is familiar with.

Additionally, discover what AT is out there in the internet world. A suggestion would be to explore the tools yourself first before introducing them to your child so that they do not become frustrated by the tool and disengaged from the time it may take to figure it out. Some tech tools that can be considered for your child based on their strengths, limitations, experiences, the concept being learned, and where they are learning can be found in

Table 8.1 later, with additional tech tools listed in the resources section of this chapter:

Consider Ease of Use

As you determine the tech tool, think of the ease of use. Will your child be capable of using the tool independently? Check out Perkins School for the Blind's Digital Math Skill Checklists to determine if your child has the age-appropriate digital math skills to be successful in math using a variety of technology tools at https://www.perkins.org/resource/digital-math-introducing-skill-level-checklists/#manipulatives. If your child has the developmental skills to use the tech tool, they are far more likely to use it unless it creates more work for them.

TABLE 8.1 Types Assistive or Instructional Technology for Mathematics Learning

Low-Level AT/Instructional Technology	High-Level AT/Instructional Technology
Graph paper—your child can use graph paper to help them write numbers evenly with a set of four boxes. Graph paper can also be used to create arrays for multiplication or to support aligning numbers in the correct place value column. It can also be used for graphing functions and drawing shapes or diagrams.	**Digital graph paper**—Your child can download virtual graph paper and explore the capabilities of the program. Math keyboards can also assist students in writing (https://virtual-graph-paper.com/ or https://print-graph-paper.com/virtual-graph-paper).
Manipulatives—Your child can use a variety of manipulatives to support the learning through the use of concrete materials. Manipulatives can vary based on the concept (counters can include commercial counters like bears or pompom balls from a craft store to dried beans; rulers; fraction circles; number lines, dominoes, fraction strips; clocks; base ten blocks; geoboards; protractors; pattern shapes, money; etc.).	**Digital or Virtual Manipulatives**—Your child will be able to use brightly colored digital/virtual manipulatives that look similar to ones used in a lesson at school but are available for your child whenever they feel the need to use manipulatives as well as to reinforce skills. Didax and Polypad provide a variety of virtual manipulatives.

(Continued)

TABLE 8.1 (Continued)

Low-Level AT/Instructional Technology	High-Level AT/Instructional Technology
Calculators—your child can use a calculator for checking their answers or promoting accuracy and quickness in solving simple or complex problems. Calculators with large number and symbol buttons may be more helpful for small fingers and to reduce error in touching a key/button.	**Graphing Calculators, Talking Calculators, and Digital Calculators, Computers/Laptops, iPads/Tablets, and Cellular Devices**—Calculators help in solving problems accurately. A jumbo talking calculator will provide your child with large, easy-to-see buttons or keys to press and voice-over of buttons pressed. Scientific calculators have graphing capabilities that provide your child with a way to double check their work or even help them to understand how the graph should look. Computers have built-in AT and can also be used to download or access apps and programs that provide your child math learning activities.
Games—Your child can practice math skills playing board games, card games, sorting objects, or even simple homemade math games focused on a specific skill or concept.	**Computer Software Games or Apps**—Computer technology games and apps can be helpful in building your child's understanding of mathematics operations. They can practice skills such as addition, subtraction, multiplication, and division in a fun and engaging way while building towns or fighting monsters.

Build in Positive Reinforcement

If your child is using an AT tool, positively reinforce them for using the tool. Because using an AT device may require an extra step to get the device and use it; for example, a talking calculator. You want to encourage and reinforce your child for taking that additional step. Build in a reward system for your child while they work using software programs or apps that build fluency and accuracy. If the app or software has a gaming-type approach, ask about where they are in the game (building a town, defeating monsters, etc.), or even take time and watch them (play) learn. Your time and attention is also a reward.

Read, Watch, and Learn

- Explore the Pacer Center Champions for Children with Disabilities (PACER) Center, which is an organization that supports parents of children with disabilities. The have a lending library for AT devices and a list of math resources to explore at Pacer.org. https://www.pacer.org/webinars/ATforRWM/MathResources.pdf
- The Simon Technology Center of PACER hosts a YouTube channel which has several videos of different AT/IT supports for math. They provide demonstrations of some of the tools, which is helpful to see how the tech tools work to support your child. https://www.youtube.com/@pacerstc
- Viewing math tutorials is another way to use technology tools available should you or your child need to review a mathematics concept. Khan Academy Kids hosts several tutorial videos that are visually helpful to review math concepts. https://www.khanacademy.org/

Summary

Successful and effective use of technology for the teaching and learning of mathematics depends upon sound teaching and learning strategies that come from an understanding of the effects of technology on mathematics education. Technology can provide a way for students to visualize math concepts. Since technology is continuously evolving it is important to understand what the AT or IT tool is doing for your child and whether or not your child enjoys using it and finds it effective.

Resources

https://teacher.desmos.com/ Desmos—free interactive K-12 lessons

https://dyscalculiaservices.com/happy-hundreds-help-with-math-facts/ Happy Hundreds help with math facts can help students visualize sets of arrays in multiplication

https://www.mathlearningcenter.org/apps The Math Learning Center shares a variety of free apps based on visual models that are available in different versions both web-based and downloadable

https://www.mathspad.co.uk/resources.php?interactives=1 MathsPad Interactive Tools

https://www.mathletics.com/us/ Mathletics-personalized learning math programs

https://www.ixl.com/ IXL—K12 personalized learning

https://www.didax.com/math/virtual-manipulatives.html?srsltid=AfmBOoq2BEomB_YjBmuGo2d-4fnMi_7JZmrtbF6nFeTBWllcgv628tR6 Didax (Virtual Manipulatives)-

http://nlvm.usu.edu/en/nav/vlibrary.html National Library of Virtual Manipulatives

https://polypad.amplify.com/p Polypad (Virtual manipulatives)

https://toytheater.com/category/teacher-tools/virtual-manipulatives/ Toy Theatre Virtual Manipulatives

Free Online Textbooks, Flashcards, Adaptive Practice, Real World Examples, Simulations (*www.ck12.org*) CK12 AI Tutor

https://do2learn.com/activities/mathhelpers/index.htm Do2learn Printable Math Grid

https://www.photomath.net Photomath—step by step explanations

https://www.modmath.com/ Modmath—assistive technology for math that helps students with dyslexia, dysgraphia, and other learning differences write and solve math problems

References

Abdelwahab, M. M., Al-Karawi, K. A., & Semary, H. E. (2025). A systematic review of assistive technology for enhancing students with disabilities. *Journal of Disability Research*, 4(2), 20240117. https://doi.org/10.57197/JDR-2024-0117

Akpan, J. P., & Beard, L. A. (2014). Assistive technology and mathematics education. *Universal Journal of Educational Research*, *2*(3), 219–222. https://doi.org/10.13189/ujer.2014.020311

Boaler, J. (2014). Research suggests that timed tests cause math anxiety. *Teaching Children Mathematics*, *20*(8), 469–474. https://doi.org/10.5951/teacchilmath.20.8.0469

Kaur, J., Abdul Majid, R., & Abdul Wahab, N. (2018). Adaptive web-based learning courseware for students with *Dyscalculia*. In *International Conference on User Science and Engineering*, 148–159.

National Council of Teachers of Mathematics (2023). *Equitable Integration of Technology for Mathematics Learning: A position of the National Council of Teachers of Mathematics.* https://www.nctm.org/standards-and-positions/equitable-integration-of-technology/

Picha, G. (2018, October). Effective technology use in math class: Ensuring that the technology we bring into math classes fosters active engagement is key. *Edutopia*. https://www.edutopia.org/article/effective-technology-use-math-class/

Raskind, M. (2013). Assistive technology. *Infographic from Council for Learning Disabilities.* https://www.council-for-learning-disabilities.org/wp-content/uploads/2013/11/AssistiveTechnology.pdf

U.S.Congress. (2004). Individuals with Disabilities Education Improvement Act of 2004. *Public Law*, 108–446. https://www.congress.gov/bill/108th-congress/house-bill/1350/text

9
Effective School Plans

Effective School Plans Explained

As introduced in Chapter 7, federal legislation affords certain protections to students with disabilities to ensure they receive an equitable and free public education. If your child is failing to make adequate progress in the general education curriculum due to the challenges associated with dyscalculia, there are two avenues for accessing school-based support that you may want to explore (i.e., an Individual Education Program [IEP] or a 504 plan). To help you navigate which school plan may be appropriate for your child, we will begin by describing the laws that govern each of these two support plans and the rights they provide you and your child. We will also detail the different documents associated with each school plan and the scope of services and/or supports each provides.

The Individual Education Program (IEP)
An IEP is a legally binding document that details the specialized instruction and individualized supports that will be provided to students with eligible disabilities within a public school system. It serves as a written agreement between teachers, parents, administrators, and other school personnel on how they will work as a team to improve a child's involvement and participation in the

academic and social life of the school (see Chapter 10—Collaborating with Professionals).

- **The IEP serves two overarching purposes:**
  - To determine specific annual goals for the child
  - To detail the special education and related services, as well as any supplementary aids and supports that will be provided to the child
- **The IEP focuses on three general areas related to school life:**
  - The general education curriculum (e.g., math, science, etc.)
  - Extracurricular activities (e.g., recess, after-school programming)
  - Non-academic activities (e.g., voluntary programming such as clubs, sports)

The Individuals With Disabilities Education Act (IDEA)

IDEA (2004) is the federal law that public schools are mandated to follow in all procedures related to special education services for students in public school systems that receive federal funds. IDEA dictates who is eligible for special education services, what procedures need to be followed in determining eligibility, and the provision of services for students found eligible.

There are six provisions of IDEA:

- **A free and appropriate public education (FAPE)**—families should incur no expense for any service provided.
- **An appropriate evaluation**—when a disability is suspected a non-discriminatory evaluation must be conducted by trained professionals.
- **An Individualized Education Plan (IEP)**—Information gathered through evaluation is used to develop a specialized and individualized intervention plan.
- **Participation in the "least restrictive environment" (LRE)**—protection of the right to learn alongside their

peers without disabilities in the general education environment to the extent appropriate or alternative placements that go from least to most restrictive.
- **Parent participation**—parents have a decision-making role equal to school professionals throughout the special education process (evaluation, placement, etc.).
- **Procedural Safeguards**—enforces the rights of children and their parents (right to review all records, prior notice of meetings, placement changes, etc.).

The IEP Process

IDEA requires schools adhere to specific policies and procedures within a designated timeline. The following figure depicts the steps all public schools must follow when a student is suspected to have a qualifying disability.

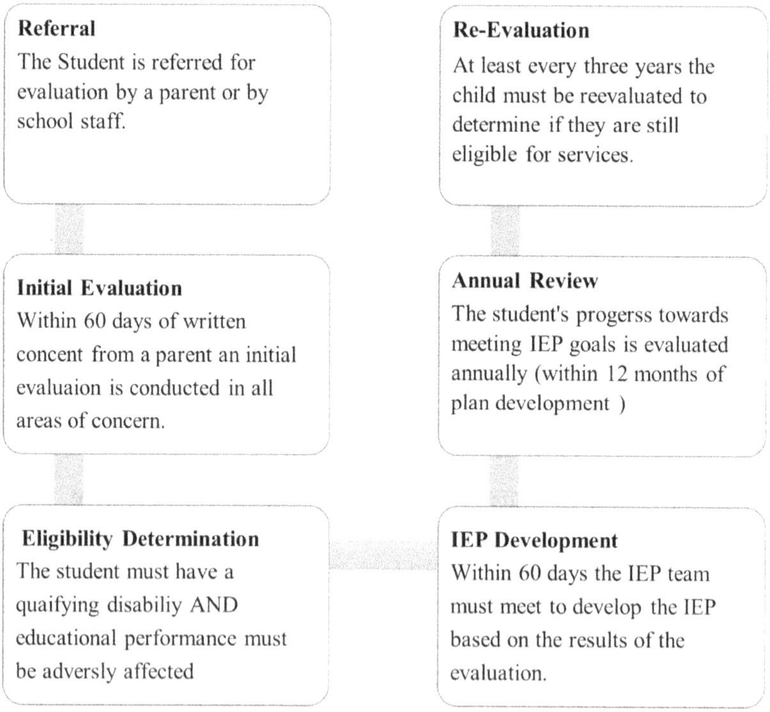

Referral
The Student is referred for evaluation by a parent or by school staff.

Initial Evaluation
Within 60 days of written concent from a parent an initial evaluaion is conducted in all areas of concern.

Eligibility Determination
The student must have a quaifying disabiliy AND educational performance must be adversly affected

Re-Evaluation
At least every three years the child must be reevaluated to determine if they are still eligible for services.

Annual Review
The student's progerss towards meeting IEP goals is evaluated annually (within 12 months of plan development)

IEP Development
Within 60 days the IEP team must meet to develop the IEP based on the results of the evaluation.

FIGURE 9.1 The Special Education Process

IDEA Requires the Following Components of the IEP:

- Present levels of performance: How your child is doing prior to intervention.
- Annual goals: What your child is expected to achieve within the year.
- Special education services: The types of services your child will receive.
- Accommodations and/or modifications: Adjustments to the learning environment or instructional methods to help your child learn differently.
- Progress monitoring: How your child's progress toward annual goals will be measured.
- Transition services: Support for transitioning to post-secondary education or the workforce (age 16 or younger).

The 504 Plan

If your child would be successful with only some reasonable adjustments made to the learning environment (such as the types of accommodations discussed in Chapter 7), then a 504 plan may be the right fit. Whereas an IEP includes specialized instruction and individualized goals to help children keep pace in the general education curriculum, a 504 plan provides accommodations but is a bit less involved, and the process to accessing one is considerably less restrictive.

Section 504 of the Rehabilitation Act of 1973. Although a 504 plan does not technically fall under the "special education" umbrella, it too is a legally binding document. Section 504 of the Rehabilitation Act of 1973 is a federal civil rights law that prevents discrimination against people with disabilities in programs that receive federal funding (e.g., public or publicly funded private schools). Section 504 defines disability more broadly than IDEA. To be eligible for 504 protections, a child must

- attend a program that receives federal funding;
- have a physical or mental impairment;
- have an impairment that substantially limits one or more life activities (e.g., learning); and

♦ have a record of that impairment, or is regarded by others to have the impairment.

The determination of whether a student has a qualifying impairment is made on an individual, and somewhat less formal basis, as the law itself does not provide great specificity on who should meet criteria for protection under Section 504. It will be up to you and your school team (see Chapter 10—Collaborating with Professionals) to discuss the extent to which your child's dyscalculia "substantially limits" your child's learning and whether a 504 plan may help remove the barriers that result from these limitations. Consider the questions posed in Chapter 7 when evaluating the extent to which your child is struggling in both the home and school environment and if they might benefit from an accommodation plan.

The 504 Process

Section 504 does not require an arduous eligibility process. On the contrary, schools often recommend a 504 plan for students who do not meet the criteria for special education services but still warrant some reasonable accommodations to be successful in the general education curriculum. You as the parent can request a 504 plan, and the school will assemble a knowledgeable team to assess if your child qualifies and, if so, what support may be needed. Although a full evaluation is not required, sources such as your child's medical diagnosis, school records, and teachers' observations and impressions will be considered.

The 504 Coordinator

Section 504 requires each school district to have a designated 504 coordinator. This role is typically assigned to an administrator (e.g., principal, vice-principal), however it can be any school employee that is knowledgeable about federal and state discrimination laws. The name and contact information for the 504 coordinator at your child's school should be available on their official website.

Parents' Rights Under Section 504:
- The school district must provide you with written notification of Section 504 protections
- You have the right to prior notice of any actions related to identification, evaluation, or placement
- You have the right to prior notice when the school is changing or discontinuing services for their child
- You have the right to access and review all of your child's records
- You have the right to participate in an impartial hearing and review process to address grievances
- You have the right to file a complaint with Office for Civil Rights (OCR) of the Department of Education

Benefits of 504 Plans:
- Legally acknowledges the disability
- Provides accommodations without altering expectations
- Applicable to all settings
- Often easier and faster to put in place
- Can reduce pressure, anxiety

Limitations of 504 Plans:
- It does not require parental involvement
- It does not require a comprehensive evaluation
- It does not require a detailed written document
- There are no strict timelines
- There are no progress monitoring requirements

Is an IEP or a 504 plan right for your child? That is a question that is best answered by an interdisciplinary team that is knowledgeable about the laws and your child. When determining the level of support your child may need, consider the differences between the two types of school plans discussed here, and know yours and your child's rights within each process.

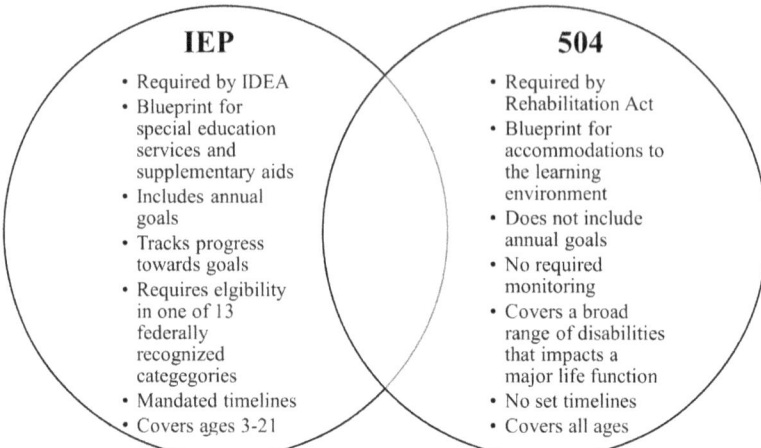

FIGURE 9.2 IEPs vs 504 Plans at a Glance

What the Research Reports

The Role of Teachers in School Plans

Research shows that educators' ability to write effective IEPs improves with experience and that ongoing professional development is essential to support and strengthen these competencies over time. In 2024, Mckenna and colleagues conducted a systematic review of the scholarly research focused on the characteristics and/or quality of IEPs for students with learning disabilities. The author group reported the following concerns consistently observed across the reviewed studies:

- Incomplete Present Levels of Academic Achievement and Functional Performance (PLAAFPs)
- Absence of goals that target student needs
- Lack of specificity in accommodations to sufficiently inform classroom implementation
- Limited parental involvement in IEP development

The findings in this article emphasize how crucial it is for parents to be actively involved and well-informed during the

IEP writing process. It also underscores the importance of having expert support available to parents when necessary.

The Role of Parents in School Plans

Parents play a vital role in IEP goal development by providing unique insights into their child's strengths, needs, and priorities. Their active participation ensures that goals are both meaningful and well-aligned with their child's real-world and long-term outcomes. In 2019, Kurth et al. examined the extent to which parent input was incorporated into critical components of the IEP, including the writing of annual goals. Despite parents' clear articulation of their concerns and recognition of their child's strengths, these meaningful contributions were often insufficiently reflected in the finalized IEP goals and services. In about one-third of the cases, the concerns and priorities shared by parents were not matched with any specific goals or services. In some instances, the goals and services included in the IEP seemed to contradict what parents had expressed.

Although this study did not focus on the learning disability population specifically, the reported findings have implications for all parents who serve in an advocacy role and are concerned with the appropriateness of their child's goals. The authors reiterate the mandate for parent participation by IDEA and caution educational teams from limiting parents' roles as signers of the document or relying on "just a checkbox or signature that they were present" (Kurth et al., 2019, p. 495).

The Role of Students in School Plans

Beyond highlighting the importance of parental involvement in shared decision making, research also emphasizes the value of engaging students in the development of their own IEP goals and in identifying the supports most appropriate to their success. Martin et al. (2006) investigated a framework for student involvement in IEP meetings that emphasized collaboration among students, their families, and school personnel. The researchers showed that when students actively participate in developing their own goals and articulating their own needs, they develop improved self-awareness, stronger advocacy skills, and higher levels of motivation. In turn, these students were better prepared for the transition to post-secondary settings and exhibited longer-term self-determination skills.

Quick Start Guide to Effective School Plans

Now that you are up to speed about the laws that govern school-based services and have an understanding of what purpose each educational plan serves, you will be better prepared to advocate for the most effective school plan for your child. However, it is not uncommon for even the most knowledgeable parents to encounter some bumps in the road when navigating through the legal processes and procedures described here. To help prevent potential roadblocks that could delay your child's access to appropriate supports, we will provide practical strategies for identifying any missing or incomplete components that could compromise the effectiveness of each school plan.

Common Roadblocks to Effective IEPS
- Failure to include all required IEP components
- Failure to include a full description of a student's needs in the Present Levels of Academic Achievement and Functional Performance (PLAAFP)
- Failure to develop annual goals based on student needs
- Failure to include appropriate, ambitious, and measurable annual goals
- Failure to provide adequate special education services
- Failure to provide special education and related services that are evidence-based
- Failure to monitor the student's progress toward annual goals
- Failure to put programming ahead of placement (how rather than where the child will receive support services

Roadmap to More Effective IEPs

Even with the best intentions, educational teams can sometimes make mistakes or overlook important details. It is important to identify and correct them quickly to ensure your child receives an appropriate support plan. You can help by getting yourself familiarized with what a solid support plan looks like. Before meeting with your educational team, request a blank copy of the IEP document used by your district and spend a few minutes locating where each of the IDEA required components can be found. The look of each document will vary between school districts, but the required content will be the same. As you locate each section, jot down any questions you have and make note of any requests or recommendations you want to share in future discussions. Having a "blank roadmap" will help you navigate through the written plan you will receive after meeting with your team. This is a draft, not a fixed document. If any of the required IEP components are missing or unclear in the draft copy provided, then you can and should request that revisions be made. If needed, enlist the support of another knowledgeable parent or advocate to help you review the document. You can train yourself to have a keen eye for seeing what is missing if you have the right support.

A strong IEP clearly shows where your child is now in terms of performance and sets specific goals for where the team wants your child to be by the end of the year. If there is no discernable path between point A and point B, then the team still has some work to do! To help you develop a keen eye for reviewing your child's IEP, we will highlight two key acronyms that focus on two of its most important components.

A Clear Starting Point: PLAAFPs

IDEA requires that every IEP include a statement of the student's Present Levels of Academic Achievement and Functional Performance (PLAAFP). PLAAFP statements should be based on comprehensive data collected from previous evaluations, standardized assessments, teacher observations, and all other relevant sources. The PLAAFP (Present Levels of Academic Achievement and Functional Performance) should guide both the selection and the wording of your child's annual goals. When reviewing PLAAFP statements look for the following: When reviewing your child's PLAAFP statements, look for the following key elements:

- A description of the student's academic (e.g., math) and/or functional (e.g., behavior, communication) needs (both strengths and weaknesses).
- Documentation of the student's current levels of performance prior to introduction of the IEP (baseline data).
- A statement on how the student's disability affects participation and/or progress in the general education curriculum.
- A clear justification for the goals, services, and supports outlined in the IEP.

Box 9.1   Example of A PLAAFP Statement for Math

Dylan demonstrates difficulty understanding the concept of place value, which adversely affects his ability to consistently and accurately perform tasks involving multi-digit numbers in both math computations and word problems. Despite targeted interventions, including small-group instruction, computerized practice programs, Dylan continues to struggle to understand the value of digits in numbers based on their position (ones, tens, hundreds, etc.). Specifically, Dylan has difficulty when working with numbers larger than 100. Dylan is often unable to correctly identify the value of digits in positions beyond the tens place. Dylan requires additional guidance to align numbers by place value, frequently making errors in carrying or borrowing. Despite these challenges, Dylan is able to understand mathematical concepts when presented with concrete, hands-on learning tools such as manipulatives or visual aids. He excels in tasks involving patterns and visual organization of information, such as geometry and measurement when visual representations are provided.

- **S** — **Specific**: Should be clear and concise, leaving no room for interpretation.
- **M** — **Measurable:** Should be observable/have specific criteria for mastery.
- **A** — **Action Verbs**: Should name observable behaviors (The student should be able to...count, solve, calulate etc.)
- **R** — **Realistic:** Should be practical, ambitious, attainable
- **T** — **Time-Limited**: Should have a specified timeline for mastery

FIGURE 9.3 SMART Goals Acronym

A Clear Destination: SMART Goals

Now that we have a clear understanding of Dylan's current levels of performance prior to the development of his IEP, the next step is to determine his goals for the year. It is essential to establish measurable annual goals that outline what Dylan is expected to achieve. Sometimes IEP goals aren't written clearly or specifically enough to easily track a child's progress, which can make it harder to quickly determine if the plan is effective. You can use the SMART acronym as a simple visual checklist to review and ensure the quality of the goals written in your child's IEP.

Let's Practice.... Is the Following Goal SMART?

Box 9.2   Practicing Identifying A SMART Goal

By the end of the first reporting period (September–December), Dylan will correctly identify and place values of multi-digit numbers (up to 100) with 80 percent accuracy in four out of five trials, using a place value chart.

Let's Break it Down:
- It is Specific. . . . Yes, it focuses on place value of multi-digit numbers.
- It is Measurable. . . . Yes, it sets a clear criterion of 80 percent accuracy in four out of five trials.
- It is Achievable. . . . Yes, it states support of a visual aid from a student's accommodation list.
- It is Relevant. . . . Yes, it targets an area of need identified in the PLAAFP.
- It is Time-Limited. . . . Yes, it clearly states criterion is to be met by the end of the first reporting period.

More Examples of SMART Goals for Dyscalculia:
- By the end of the first reporting period (September–December), the student will accurately tell time to the nearest five minutes on an analog clock in four out of five trials, with the use of time-telling strategies and visual aids.
- By the end of the semester, (January–June), the student will independently solve one-step word problems involving addition or subtraction with 80 percent accuracy on weekly probes, using a graphic organizer.
- By the end of the academic year, the student will accurately solve ten out of 12 single-digit addition and subtraction problems within five minutes, with no more than one error per session.
- Within three months, the student will answer 15 out of 20 multiplication or division facts (up to five times) with 90 percent accuracy in three-minute timed drills without the use of a visual aid.
- By the end of the first grading period, the student will independently use a graphic organizer to plan and solve word problems in math with at least 80 percent accuracy, as evidenced by teacher observation and accuracy of assignment probes.

Common Roadblocks to Effective 504s
- Not exploring the breadth of supports that can be provided in a 504 plan

- Not notifying the student that you want to be involved in all meetings
- Accepting a "one-size-fits all" plan used for students with the same disability
- Taking a "kitchen sink approach" to listing accommodations
- Assuming teachers have been notified that a 504 has recently been put in place
- Assuming the school will implement the plan consistently across teachers, classes, time

Roadmap to Effective 504 Plans

- Check that the Disability is Documented Clearly and Accurately: Clear documentation helps the school understand the specific needs and provide appropriate support.
- Document in Writing: Ensure that all agreed-upon accommodations and supports are documented formally.
- Check that Accommodations are Individualized: Make sure they are practical and appropriate for your child's age and unique learning needs.

TABLE 9.1 Non-Examples and Examples of Specific Accommodations in a 504 Plan

Too Vague	More Specific
Give extended time	Provide 50 percent extended time on all timed assessments
Provide visual aids	Use of place value charts, mnemonic devices for order of operations, formula cheat sheet
Allow breaks	Allow a five- to ten-minute break between assessments
Support organization	Provide the student color-coded folders or binders for different types of math materials.
Provide homework support	Break down math homework into smaller, more manageable sections, and provide written instructions with examples
Provide encouragement	Use of a daily positive reinforcement system to encourage task completion (not accuracy)

- Check that Accommodations are Specific: Clarify any vague language—specify exactly what accommodations will be provided and when.
- Invite Feedback from Your Child: Ask how they feel about the accommodations—and what might need to be added or improved.

Summary

In Chapter 9, we provide a clear roadmap to help you navigate school-based support services for the first time. You learned about the rights granted to you and your child under federal laws, and we'll guide you on how to advocate effectively for the right school plan—at the right time and for the right reasons. We also highlight common roadblocks many parents face during plan development and equip you with practical tips to overcome these barriers, ensuring your child receives the support they need, exactly when they need it. In Chapter 10, we'll prepare you to work respectfully and collaboratively with school staff, helping ensure that both you and your child feel heard, valued, and supported throughout the process.

Resources

https://www2.ed.gov/about/offices/list/ocr/504faq.html U.S. Department of Education, Office for Civil Rights (OCR)

https://www.understood.org/en/articles/504-plan-overview Understood.Org 504 Plans

https://iris.peabody.vanderbilt.edu/module/iep/ Developing High-Quality Individualized Education Programs

https://www.wrightslaw.com/info/sec504.index.htm Wrightslaw—Information Section 504

References

Kurth, J. A., McQueston, J. A., Ruppar, A. L., Samantha, G. T., Johnston, R., & McCabe, K. M. (2019). A description of parent input in IEP development through analysis IEP documents. *Intellectual and Developmental Disabilities*, *57*(6), 485–498. https://doi.org/10.1352/1934-9556-57.6.485

Martin, J. E., Van Dycke, J. L., Christensen, W. R., & Greene, B. A. (2006). Increasing student participation in IEP meetings: Establishing the self-directed IEP as an evidence-based practice. *Exceptional Children*, *72*(3), 299–316. https://doi.org/10.1177/001440290607200304

10

Collaborating With Professionals

Collaborating With Professionals Explained

Effective intervention for your child with dyscalculia requires open and ongoing collaboration between you and your school team. Each team member you work with, be it a general education teacher, a special educator, a school psychologist, or a math specialist will bring unique expertise and valuable perspectives to the table. In the popular Post Malone and Morgan Wallen song, "I Had Some Help" they sing "Teamwork makes the dream work." By working together, you and your school team can do more than dream. You'll develop strong educational plans that are tailored to your child's unique learning needs and allow for more coordinated support across learning environments.

As your child's first and most steady advocate, building strong partnerships with the specialists supporting your child is essential to fostering trust and reducing feelings of overwhelm over time. In this final chapter, we will support you in becoming both a confident advocate and a collaborative partner as you navigate your child's journey with dyscalculia across settings and time.

Advocating in Public vs. Private School Settings

From previous chapters, you have become more familiar with the federal laws (IDEA and Section 504 of the Rehabilitation Act) that determine how school-based support services are accessed and delivered and what level of support each connected plan (IEPs and 504s) can potentially provide your child. You also gained a greater understanding of your and your child's rights, as well as how school plans are designed to protect you both from determining eligibility, to developing the plan, to implementing it and monitoring progress. Here, we will help inform your decision making as you consider what educational setting and what support plan may be best suited for you and your child.

IDEA and IEPs
Since the majority of private schools do not receive federal funding, they are not obligated to comply with IDEA or provide an Individualized Education Program (IEP) for students with disabilities enrolled in their programs. This also means that if you choose to transfer your child from a public to a private school, the new school will not be obligated to honor and implement the IEP. Whereas some private schools may offer some degree of support services—such as academic tutoring or access to a learning specialist—these services are offered at the school's discretion, rather than mandated by federal legislation.

However, there are exceptions to this rule. If your chosen private school receives any federal financial assistance, either directly or through your local public school system, then the school may be obligated to comply with certain provisions of IDEA. There are some specialized private schools that serve students with disabilities that may fall under this category. Or, if a public school places your child in a private setting because it is unable to meet their complex needs, then their rights under IDEA (i.e., FAPE) will remain protected, and your child will be supported by an IEP. The latter is a rare circumstance.

Section 504 and 504 plans
As you may recall, Section 504 of the Rehabilitation Act prohibits discrimination on the basis of disability in any program or activity that receives federal funds from the U.S. Department of Education. These protections extend to public school districts, colleges and universities, and other local and state education agencies including some private schools that receive funds directly or

indirectly (e.g., federal school lunch programs, programs for at-risk students, educational reform grants, etc.). For recipients of federal funds, public or private, the mandated protections under 504 will remain the same across settings. This means your child may be eligible for reasonable accommodations in both public and private schools, which could broaden the range of educational options available to you.

However, keep in mind, the level of support school teams can offer for dyscalculia varies and should be carefully explored. Later in the chapter, we will provide you with strategies for evaluating school programs for your child and will discuss how to advocate differently but just as diligently in public vs. private school settings.

Working With a Private Tutor

No matter which school program you choose, many parents find it necessary to work with a private tutor to help their child with dyscalculia keep up or catch up academically. The many benefits parents find when hiring a private tutor include flexible scheduling, undivided 1:1 attention, slower pacing, immediate feedback and reinforcement, and improved confidence. If you have the time and resources to invest in a private tutor for your child, be sure to choose one that has a background in special education, specialized training in dyscalculia, and has the patience and wherewithal to adapt to your child's strengths and needs. Consider posing the following questions to potential tutors before making any hiring decisions:

- What is your experience working with students who struggle with (list your child's identified areas of concerns; e.g., number sense, solving word problems, etc.)?
- How do you tailor your instruction to address individualized IEP annual goals? Incorporate their specific accommodations?
- What does a typical session look like?
- How will progress be monitored, and how often will it be communicated?

♦ Do you collaborate and assist with families working with IEP or 504 teams?

In the remaining chapter, we will provide you with research-based information for the rationale for tutoring and collaboration, promoting positive home-school communication, and how to find and work with private tutors in a wrap-around support model.

What the Research Reports

Educational research documents the significant impact of collaboration, tutoring, and school-based collaborative instructional approaches on improving mathematics achievement among students. When parents and teachers work as active collaborators it leads to better academic, behavioral, and developmental outcomes for children (Garbacz et al., 2022). Effective strategies include establishing two-way communication, shared decision making, and relational partnerships built on equality. As discussed in previous chapters, obtaining the most from the MTSS process also requires parent and professional collaboration. Weingarten and colleagues (2020) identified that characteristics of successful MTSS teams included helping families have a clear understanding of the MTSS process, using multidirectional communication with families, making data understandable, and viewing parents as partners in the process. They noted teacher and parent collaboration leads to better student outcomes.

Teacher-student tutoring support and collaboration in classroom learning environments also play an important role in fostering a student's mathematical understanding and performance. Tutoring, whether delivered in person or online, has consistently demonstrated positive effects on students' math outcomes. Beal et al. (2007) found that intelligent online tutoring systems that offer adaptive feedback can significantly improve students' performance on standardized math tests. Similarly, Topping et al. (2011), in a randomized controlled trial, showed that structured math tutoring, especially for lower-performing students, leads to substantial academic gains. Jehadus et al. (2022) further emphasized that the effectiveness of tutoring was enhanced when combined with strong student motivation where motivated learners benefited from individualized instructional support.

In addition to the collaboration from tutoring, when teachers use collaborative practices with each other, it has the potential to create higher mathematics achievement. Ronfeldt et al. (2015) and Saka (2021) both found that when teachers engage in regular, instructionally focused collaboration, student achievement improves due to better planning, sharing of best practices, and collective problem solving. These findings support collaboration between teachers has the potential to improve their students' educational outcomes.

Even collaboration among students can improve math performance. Siller and Ahmad (2024) examined collaboration among students and found that collaborative learning approaches not only improved grade six students' mathematics achievement but also positively influenced their attitudes toward math. This dual benefit highlights the value of collaboration in peer-tutoring types of learning.

Quick Start Guide to Collaborating With Professionals

While school professionals are responsible for fostering collaborative and respectful team interactions throughout the process, we also want to ensure that you feel prepared to contribute equally and effectively to a positive team culture. Above all, we're here to help you feel confident and ready to advocate effectively at each stage of the journey. So, here we offer tips and tools for working effectively with professionals in both home and school settings—so you can be assertive, respectful, and well-prepared every step of the way.

Tips for Collaborative Team Meetings

As discussed in previous chapters, even well-meaning educational teams may occasionally fall short of the high standards we encourage you to expect from them, regardless of what setting you choose for your child. Especially in the case of public schools who fall under both federally mandated laws discussed here, we want you to be on the lookout for attitudes or statements that are unlawful and/or overly biased. This includes these unfortunate experiences shared by parents:

- Dismissing their concerns
- Ignoring their child's strengths
- Discussion about budget limits
- Making generalizations
- Projecting personal bias
- Using overly technical language or unexplained jargon

Being aware of these common lapses of judgment shared by others can help pave the way for improved communication, greater understanding, and more effective teamwork for you. Even when IEP meetings fall short of ideal collaboration, each one presents an opportunity to strengthen communication and partnership. Here are some steps you can take to be a prepared and collaborative advocate at your future team meetings.

Before the Meeting:
- Know the purpose of the meeting
- Know who should be in attendance
- Request a copy of all evaluation reports and/or educational records
- Request a copy of drafted goals/listed accommodations to review
- Organize documents neatly in a binder with easy-to-read tabs for quick retrieval
- Draft your vision/parent input statement to include describing specific concerns, strengths, and strategies to discuss

During the Meeting:
- Some parents like to bring a photo of their child, if not present, to personalize the experience

- Pause the discussion to ask questions, clarify jargon
- If you need to, read your prepared parent statement to ensure you get what is important to you on record
- Speak up respectfully/neutrally if a statement about your child does not ring true
- Bring a support person to help keep you focused and to take detailed note

After the Meeting
- Use provided checklists/visuals to check for all required components
- Confirm all service providers have received the new support plan
- File documents away into your binder or chosen organization system
- If you have concerns that are not easily addressed via email, phone—request an IEP meeting ahead of the annual review
- Make note in your calendar of progress monitoring dates, and have your child goals and evaluation criteria easy to reference

Tips for Effective Home School Communication

Parents who have walked this path before have found that with some effort, advocacy and collaboration can occur simultaneously and harmoniously. Below are some tips parents have shared on how they set and maintain a positive tone in their home-school communications.

- Express early your desire to collaborate as a team
- Keep a communication log (records of emails, calls, notes, etc.)
- Share insights about your child's successes and challenges at home
- Ask questions and seek clarification when jargon is used
- Follow up on concerns to ensure they are addressed
- Be solution-focused

- Acknowledge teachers' time and efforts in writing
- Encourage self-advocacy as your child grows

Tips for Locating Qualified Tutors

Finding a qualified math tutor can make a significant difference in your child's learning. Your child should like the tutor they work with, and while they are not friends, their personalities should "click," as we tend to work harder for people we like. Once you have tutor's contact information, vet them about their educational background, teaching experience with the age of your child, and obtain references to call. Even ask for a trial first session where you observe their effect, patience, pacing, and overall demeanor during the session.

Here are additional tips for locating a math tutor. Review online platforms, including the following:

- **Wyzant**—Math **and other subjects**
- **Varsity Tutors**—Offers live online and in-person options
- **Chegg Tutors**—On-demand math help
- **Tutor.com**—24/7 math and other academic support

Reach out to your local library, as many offer free or low-cost tutoring. Your local university or community college might have a list of students majoring in education or math that tutor, and don't forget to ask your child's school if they have a list of local tutors. Tutoring is expensive, but we believe it's a worthwhile and valuable investment in your child's confidence and ultimately their future.

Summary

Collaboration seems like common sense, but effective collaboration takes intentionality and time. Knowing the key players to collaborate with and having general knowledge about each person's role can help create realistic expectations. You'll have closer collaborative relationships with some professionals such as your child's teacher and tutor and less with others such as the school psychologist. Nevertheless, collaboration is shown to improve educational outcomes for students, so our advice is try not to be a lone wolf but part of a true team where differences are expected but the team is focusing on helping the MVP, your child, excel and thrive in math and more.

Resources

The following are online tutoring websites:
Wyzant.com
VarsityTutors.com
Chegg.com/study
Tutor.com

References

Beal, C. R., Walles, R., Arroyo, I., & Woolf, B. P. (2007). On-line tutoring for math achievement testing: A controlled evaluation. *Journal of Interactive Online Learning*, *6*(1), 43–55.

Garbacz, A., Godfrey, E., Rowe, D. A., & Kittelman, A. (2022). Increasing parent collaboration in the implementation of effective practices. *Teaching Exceptional Children*, *54*(5), 324–327.

Jehadus, E., Tamur, M., Chen, J., & Perbowo, K. S. (2022). The influence of tutoring and learning motivation on mathematics achievement of junior high school students. *Journal of Honai Math*, *5*(1), 75–82.

Ronfeldt, M., Farmer, S. O., McQueen, K., & Grissom, J. A. (2015). Teacher collaboration in instructional teams and student achievement. *American Educational Research Journal*, *52*(3), 475–514.

Saka, O. A. (2021). Can teacher collaboration improve students' academic achievement in junior secondary mathematics? *Asian Journal of University Education*, *17*(1), 33–46.

Siller, H. S., & Ahmad, S. (2024). Analyzing the impact of collaborative learning approach on grade six students' mathematics achievement and attitude towards mathematics. *EURASIA Journal of Mathematics, Science and Technology Education*, *20*(2), em2395.

Topping, K. J., Miller, D., Murray, P., Henderson, S., Fortuna, C., & Conlin, N. (2011). Outcomes in a randomised controlled trial of mathematics tutoring. *Educational Research*, *53*(1), 51–63.

Weingarten, Z., Zumeta Edmonds, R., & Arden, S. (2020). Better together: Using MTSS as a structure for building school–family partnerships. *Teaching Exceptional Children*, *53*(2), 122–130.

For Product Safety Concerns and Information please contact our EU representative GPSR@taylorandfrancis.com
Taylor & Francis Verlag GmbH, Kaufingerstraße 24, 80331 München, Germany

www.ingramcontent.com/pod-product-compliance
Lightning Source LLC
Chambersburg PA
CBHW050644160426
43194CB00010B/1803